Management Science in
Federal Agencies

Management Science in Federal Agencies

The Adoption and Diffusion of a Socio-Technical Innovation

Michael J. White
Syracuse University

JF
1411
W45

Lexington Books
D.C. Heath and Company
Lexington, Massachusetts
Toronto   London

Library of Congress Cataloging in Publications Data

White, Michael, 1942-
  Management science in Federal agencies.

  Includes bibliographical references and index.

  1. Public administration. 2. Management. 3. United States
—Executive department—Management. I. Title.
JF1411.W45   353   74-16946
ISBN 0-669-95927-8

Copyright © 1975 by D.C. Heath and Company

Published simultaneously in Canada

Printed in the United States of America

International Standard Book Number: 0-669-95927-8

Library of Congress Catalog Card Number: 74-16946

Contents

List of Figures

List of Tables

Preface

To some people, the study of public administration seems backward because of a scarcity of behavioral theory and empirical research. Perhaps the proper inference from these weaknesses is that the significant phenomena do not yield easily to current research methods and that students of public administration are still close enough to the people they study to resist trading relevance for elegance. The development of management science activities is typical of many interesting phenomena in public administration, in that this development involves processes that are revealed over a period of several years. Further, management scientists may not leave behind adequately descriptive archival records.

It has been possible for me to study management science activities in many agencies as they developed over almost five years because of the intellectual vision or generosity or patience—or sometimes all three combined—of a large number of people. First among these is Michael Radnor of Northwestern University, who stimulated, encouraged, and assisted my thinking and who generously helped with financial support from his N.A.S.A. grant #NGL-14-007-058 and from his grant from the Booz Allen Hamilton Foundation. Harold Guetzkow, who chaired the committee which supervised the Ph.D. dissertation on which this book is based, encouraged rigor, discipline, and professionalism. Albert H. Rubenstein and his Program of Research on the Management of Research and Development at Northwestern provided an intellectual and administrative home in the beginning. David A. Tansik was an indispensable colleague and intellectual companion throughout the fieldwork period. Alden S. Bean spent many nights with me, searching for order. Harry Welsch contributed importantly to the fieldwork and critically to the coding of data. Richard T. Barth and Michael Burstein also made contributions to the fieldwork. Fred Vetter clarified my thinking on more occasions than he knows; I owe a special debt to him. Numberless, unnamed field respondents gave their time, trust, and concerned interest; one could ask no more from government than that it always be staffed by people of such character and intellect. In addition to Dr. Radnor, administrative support has been provided by Sidney Ulmer and Malcolm Jewell (the University of Kentucky), Robert T. Golembiewski (the University of Georgia), and Frank Marini and James D. Carroll (Syracuse University) and their staffs.

Judith F. White always stayed close in spite of provocation, transcending patience. For her, most of all, and for the others, I am fortunate.

1 Introduction

Management science has received skeptical attention from social scientists in recent years. The claims of some management scientists may—but should not—lead social scientists and others interested in government decision-making to treat the management science movement lightly. The claims of management scientists are assertions about preferable ways to conduct government, and the growing application of management science in government indicates that these are not empty assertions. Management science is also a base from which a policy science might be constructed. Both for its current and its possible future impact, then, management science in government needs to be understood as a social phenomenon.

Management science is usually considered a technology, with only incidental reference to management scientists. Here, however, it is viewed as a social activity that occurs in government organizations, among other places. Through a longitudinal, comparative, field investigation, I have collected information in forty-six government agencies about the activities of management scientists and the relations of these scientists to other parts of their agencies. One result of this investigation is a descriptive phase model of the adoption of management science activities by government agencies. Another is an understanding of the diffusion of management science in organizations which, because this understanding is based on social and behavioral considerations, may make more realistic both expectations and fears about the consequences of management science technology.

I hope other researchers will be encouraged to pursue comparative field investigations of governmental phenomena by the example of this study, in which field contacts were maintained cordially with some agencies for more than four years—throughout reorganizations, personnel changes, and a change of administration.

Politics and Management Science

Some examples from the writings of management scientists show that management science as a technology is often proclaimed by its advocates as being something that can make government modern, improve the life of the citizenry, and optimize program administration. By comparison, in these proclamations, current government practices may be characterized as being completely subjective, irrational, and superannuated.

Maurice F. Ronayne, a management scientist with Defense Department experience, writes in his article, "Operations Research Can Help Public Administrators in Decision-Making":

Many public administrators today in the world still employ Eighteenth Century management tools to assist them in making Twentieth Century decisions. This is indeed unfortunate, especially since we are now living in an era which treats space exploration as an almost-common thing. . . .

But one tool, slowly but surely establishing itself as an aid to public administrators, and which offers tremendous promise as a method for obtaining better decision-making capabilities, is Operations Research. . . .[1]

Murray Weidenbaum, formerly an assistant secretary in the Treasury Department, wrote in 1966:

With the introduction of sophisticated managerial tools such as benefit/cost, cost/utility, and systems analysis generally, there will be a reduced tendency for decisions on authorizing and financing individual government programs to be made in isolation and solely on the basis of subjective, intuitive judgments. It is possible that the composition of the federal budget will shift substantially as a result.[2]

President Johnson, when announcing the introduction of PPBS into civilian agencies, stated the objective for this new "Planning and Budgeting system": "The objective of this program is simple: to use the most modern management tools so that the full promise of a finer life can be brought to every American at the least possible cost."[3]

Summarizing his introduction to *The Challenge to Systems Analysis,* a book edited by Grace Kelleher and sponsored by the Operations Research Society of America, L. Eugene Root sounds this hopeful note:

So the systems analyst is venturing into unusual territory when he offers his assistance in social problems. Nevertheless, the attempt must be made, and it is my belief that it can be helpful if done with appropriate balance. The mere fact that the total answer in a given situation cannot be laid out like a production schedule is no good excuse for refusing to make the attempt at all. Once we actually try, the resulting clarification of issues can be quite astonishing and our major efforts can be reserved for the more intractable parts of the situation.[4]

Referring to systems analysis and other management science applications in the military, Jacob Stockfish, a former analyst for both the Defense and Treasury Departments, concludes confidently: "Hence, the Defense Department management experience of the last seven years constitutes a 'case in point' that has general relevance wherever man seeks to use instruments of the state to achieve objectives."[5] Generally, this and other essays in Kelleher's book offer cautious optimism about the contribution of systems analysis and operations research to civilian government problems.

Less restraint has been exercised by management scientists working for contract research firms. From its management information systems, I.B.M. promises "Not Data ... but REALITY!", while the Nassau County (New York) Department of Welfare received a contract proposal promising " ... to aid the Welfare Department in optimizing programs, services, and resources to satisfy community needs."[6]

But academic researchers sometimes use what might be called "ambitious" language. In their abstract of a recent paper, Ward and Burton note that "the construction process ... has frequently resulted in adverse environmental effects." Initial attempts to moderate these effects of the construction industry have "resulted in replacing one form of environmental degradation with another less obvious form." Their paper "develops the idea that solutions to the problem lie in the area of management science."[7] Another paper promises estimates of the social costs of various family planning programs, as well as techniques for choosing the "optimal treatment variables for administration of a particular program ...."[8]

These claims are easy targets for political scientists versed in the intricacies of political processes and the difficulty of political change.

The authors quoted in this section are making three assertions: (1) management scientists should have a larger role in political decision-making; (2) optimization, modernity, and conformity with a particular view of scientific decision-making are appropriate criteria for political choice; and (3) management science knowledge is a basis for participation in policy-making.

These are *political* assertions about premises for and participation in government decisions. In Aaron Wildavsky's terms, these assertions involve "systems politics," not "policy politics"—rules of the game rather than outputs of the game.[9]

There is substance, as well as rhetoric, to these assertions. Management scientists are working on a wide range of government problems and policies, and management science activities have diffused widely.

In the course of field research for this study, over forty federal, civilian agency, management science staffs were identified and visited between 1967 and 1971, and new federal civilian agency staffs continued to be identified even after field research had been completed. In the first half of 1972, for example, three staffs in field offices were identified and contacted. In 1972 Dr. W. E. Cushen, then director of the Technical Analysis Division of the National Bureau of Standards, surveyed federal civilian agencies in the capitol area and found that in forty-four agencies, 322 operations research analysts were employed, fifty-two of whom worked for Cushen himself. The figure of 322, he notes, is up from twenty in 1960 and 100 in 1966, and includes only "operations research analyst" Civil Service classifications, not the many other classifications in which management scientists might be found. Twenty-eight of these agencies are listed by Cushen as having staffs performing "in-house operations research," as opposed to either "technical monitoring" or "no classification given." Overlap between Cushen's and my sample is only about 50 percent of each. Clearly, then, operations research activities are extensive in federal agencies. Combining my estimates with those of Cushen indicates that one or more operations research or management science groups existed in over forty federal civilian agencies in 1972 and that operations researchers were working in another dozen, with the evidence showing that this figure is the result of steady growth since 1960. Cushen predicts continued rapid growth in the demand for management scientists in government.[10]

Management science is also being applied to public problems by nongovernmental management scientists. A recent program for a semiannual meeting of the Operations Research Society of America provides abstracts of over sixty papers on such political topics as law enforcement and court administration; urban planning; fire department management; land, sea, and air transportation; health care planning, delivery, management, and facilities design; air and water pollution; solid waste management; mail delivery; public and higher education; manpower planning and vocational education; nutrition programs; civil service management; natural resource policies; mental health decision-making; welfare reform and income mainte- nance; and legislative redistricting.[11] Almost all of these papers were written by university or commercial researchers rather than government employees.

The outlook for the future may be indicated by educational offerings, for it is through formal training that future management scientists will emerge.[12] In the Washington, D.C. area, where gov- ernment is the major employer and few large industries that use management science exist, there are numerous courses offered in the management sciences. A recent issue of the newsletter of the Washington Operations Research Society lists over 300 courses in "operations research and allied areas in the Washington area" for spring 1974. Sixty-three of them are offered for graduate credit by government agencies such as the USDA Graduate School and the National Institutes of Health.[13] As I said, the rhetoric of manage- ment science may seem ambitious, but within federal civilian agen- cies, management science has a well-established base from which future growth and influence may be anticipated.

If some feel that management science, however extensive its use in government, will remain inadequate to the policy challenges of our time, there are others who see it as a foundation on which a policy science may grow. Yehezkel Dror writes that the technology of management science provides "a basic approach and frame of reference that is conducive to better policymaking because it em- phasizes explicit processes, holistic orientations, a readiness for innovation, and using interdisciplinary knowledge. . . ."[14] He also writes:

the experience of the management sciences in getting established as a recognized interdisciplinary field (or fields), in combining a normative orientation with a scientific attitude, and in gaining partial acceptance by policymakers constitutes an important experiment and precedent. Feed- back from this experience, and from its progress by trial and error, provides knowledge that is relevant to the problems involved in establishing a policy science.[15]

Michael Radnor suggests that the differences between management science and policy science have been overdrawn by the proponents of policy science. In a recent article he stated his opinion that management science is the best base for policy science:

We are looking for a science of the design, goal selection, and setting and management of complex open systems. We need a framework and eventually a theory of systems studies. The closest semi-professional existing grouping that has already attempted to include many of the relevant disciplines and technologies into various levels of application (and which is still actively pursuing this end) is Management Science. It is a pity to see some of the top, public, policy-oriented groups trying to act exclusively outside this still dynamic framework.[16]

Radnor recognizes that management science and the inchoate policy science have complementary strengths and concedes that the latter may be stronger in "institutional and behavioral understandings" and may offer greater "sensitivity to the subtleties of political life."[17] Policy science may be a vehicle for the further diffusion of management scientists and their methods into government agencies, which may relieve the adoption problems faced by management science.

We can view management science in a number of ways, then: as an expanding professional specialty in government, as a set of ideas about how government decisions should be made, and as a basis for a "policy science." Each view, however, implies that it is more than a technology; in the political process, management science means people and their activity as well. To evaluate the possibilities of management science as a technology, its manifestations in organizational behavior must be understood.

A Definition of Management Science

Because management science includes formal techniques, intellectual approaches, identifiable people, social activities, and social institutions—all interacting through recent history—it is difficult to establish exclusionary rules for its definition. Yehezkel Dror feels that "it is not easy to discuss the management sciences as a whole because quite a heterogeneous set of orientations, perceptions, methodologies, techniques, and tools are at one time or another covered by that term. Therefore discussion of management sciences can easily be contradicted by the statement that the disputant has in mind quite a different concept of management sciences."[18]

Radnor, whose thinking has influenced my conception of management science, comments: "As with some other such developments in the past, there is some difficulty in separating the proposed new *technologies* from the personalities, histories, goals, and skills of the *proponents;* from the 'movement' of which they have become a part; and from the profession that may be in the making."[19]

To the extent that the techniques and intellectual orientations often identified as management science may be publicly available intellectual property, management science must be defined according to its social, historical, and institutional characteristics.

In this study, *management science* refers to a social process in which there is the practice and use of a body of accumulated knowledge, methods, and techniques by individuals, alone or as members of groups and organizations, who have had training rooted in the traditions of operations research in World War II, RAND Corporation systems analyses, the industrial experiences which led to and grew out of the founding of the Institute of Management Sciences, and benefit-cost analysis efforts running back into the nineteenth century, and who tend to accept as desirable an approximation of what is commonly called "rational decision-making." Concomitantly, *management science* refers to persons and groups within government agencies which have a formal mission to use the available knowledge, methods and techniques to contribute to the resolution of problems facing the host agency. Critical to the definition of management science for this study is the relation of the social and historical aspects to the technical aspects of management science.

Outline and Objectives

In this book a model will be presented, describing the various patterns of adoption or development of management science groups in federal civilian agencies. The model will be used to explore the growth of actual management science activities in federal civilian agencies.

The discussion of the diffusion of management science activities in federal agencies should help clarify complicated organizational change processes which have not yet been observed sufficiently long in a large enough number of places. Further research, using this type of phase model, will be suggested. Finally, the longitudinal comparative method of this study will be contrasted with other approaches to studying management science.

The reader should eventually be able to see complex organization change in its full temporal extent, rather than in misleading, cross-sectional slices—all of which will advance the understanding of management science as a social, as well as technical, phenomenon.

2

First Steps Toward a Model of the Development and Adoption of Management Science Activities in Government Organizations

Management science has been adopted by and is developing in organizations. Describing this development-adoption process has required a special language which must be presented slowly. Generally I prefer the term *development* in presenting the model, while emphasizing *adoption* in interpreting federal agency experiences as a whole.

In Chapter 2 we will take the first steps toward articulating a descriptive phase model of the adoption and development of management science activities in government agencies and an operational definition of the phases of this model. "Mutual accommodation" is the organizing concept of the model, and there are five variables for defining the phases: legitimacy, skills level, aggressiveness, innovativeness, and the level of technology.

The Radnor-Rubenstein Phase Model of the Development of Management Science Activities in U.S. Business

Even in situations where management science is an adequate basis for making governmental decisions,[1] a management science activity still may not be able to contribute to government decisions because of organizational factors.[2] These organizational factors include the way in which the management science activity and its members interact with other persons and offices within an agency. The relations between a management science activity and others in its host organization have been the subject of varied, if not extensive, study. Specifically, the relations that occur in the implementation of management science recommendations have been studied through laboratory experiment,[3] field research,[4] formal theorizing,[5] field surveys,[6] and the reflection of experienced practitioners of management science.[7] More recently, proponents of "policy analysis" have expressed similar concern with implementation.[8]

Rubenstein and Radnor proposed an alternate approach to the study of the organizational relations of management science activities.[9] This approach involves consideration of these organizational relations in a wider context than that offered by the implementation of specific recommendations. Instead of focusing on specific transactions or events, they suggest viewing the "integration" of management science into an agency as a dynamic process to be accomplished over a period of several years. Within this period there will be many events, transactions, and recommendations for implementation. By viewing the organizational relations of a management science activity in this temporally larger perspective, Rubenstein and Radnor are consistent with the spirit of the "systems approach,"[10] which urges that problems be studied not by decomposition but by examination of a problem in its wider environment.

The Radnor-Rubenstein Phases

Rubenstein and Radnor propose a phase model of the integration of management science into an organization. In their model integration takes place in a sequence of "lifecycle" phases.[11]

First, there is a *prebirth* phase. In this phase, two activities may occur: key managers in the organization become aware of management science through personal and media experiences, and some of them begin to advocate the initiation of management science activities. At the same time, there may be mathematically trained staff or other personnel who, on their own or with some executive sponsorship, try to conduct preliminary management science work. In recent years the existence of a contracted "feasibility study" is good evidence that the organization is in the prebirth phase.

The prebirth phase is followed by the *birth* phase in which the activity is organized as a formal unit and its members go to work. This is a period of aggressive, almost missionary, behavior in which the management science analysts undertake ambitious projects and try to convert managers to a belief in the efficacy of management science. A high administrator often sponsors, protects, and provides resources for the projects.

Eventually a *decline* sets in. Management science analysts are not particularly successful in getting their projects completed and the results implemented. They run into resistance, and the administrator who sponsored the staff initially may move or leave the organization. In an attempt to win the support of potential clients, the management science analysts change their pitch and try to sell smaller, less ambitious, projects. The most highly skilled analysts may join another staff in a different organization. Sometimes the group's leader is fired outright. There is an overall decline in the professional quality of the staff, as well as the sophistication and scope of their work. This decline may continue all the way to the *death* of the staff. The staff may be abandoned and its members released or transferred within the organization.

Alternatively, the staff may survive its troubles. While key professionals are lost, they are eventually replaced, and the scope and sophistication of subsequent projects gradually increase. But this time, the relations between the staff and its clients are not those of missionary salesmen to ignorant natives. Rather, the role of the management science analyst is accepted as one involving changes based on new technologies. At the same time, the analysts become more sensitive to their clients. This is a phase of *maturity* in which management science has a stable relationship with the organization. The key idea in this model is that of an initial surge of management science activity, followed by a decline which leads either to the death of the group, or to eventual recovery leading to maturity. These ups and downs in the status of a management science activity are illustrated in Figure 2-1.

Results of a Preliminary Examination of the
Radnor-Rubenstein Phase Model

When early interview data was compared with this model, the Radnor-Rubenstein model phases appeared to fit roughly some of the government management science activities but not to fit others at all. This preliminary examination indicated that the Radnor-Rubenstein model could be used only suggestively, that a more complex model must be developed.

The preliminary examination involved transferring the data gathered in interviews conducted in 1967 and 1968 to cards according to seventeen topical categories. This information was then transferred to a large matrix of topic-versus-field-site. The question guid-

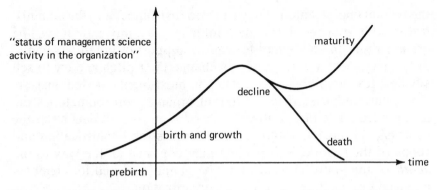

Figure 2-1. Graphical Representation of the Radnor-Rubenstein Model

ing the review was "does the history of the activity, as outlined in the interviews and other available documents, correspond to the sequenced phases of the Radnor-Rubenstein model?"

For many of the activities the expected up-and-down pattern graphed in Figure 2-1 was not found. Instead, these activities seemed to develop gradually and monotonically in size, technical capability, and acceptance.[12] The two alternatives are graphed in Figure 2-2. In a later examination of Radnor and Rubenstein's data from forty-nine industrial and business management science activities, the same conclusion was suggested, though less strongly.

The tentative conclusion was that there were two distinct patterns in the development of management science activities in organizations. The one outlined by Radnor and Rubenstein was called the "revolutionary" pattern, while the other was "evolutionary." These names were chosen to contrast the conflict, turbulence, and abrupt endings, which characterized the activities that tended to fit the Radnor-Rubenstein phases, with the more placid and harmonious process of those activities that tended not to fit their phases. The discovery of *two* patterns implied that a model with more phases might more adequately describe the development of management science activities.

Basic Concepts for a New Descriptive Model of the Development of Management Science Activities

The original phases had not been closely derived from or related to

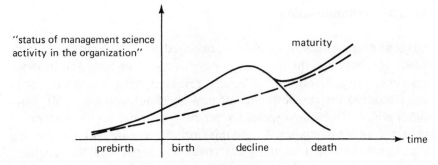

Figure 2-2. Two Alternative Patterns in the Development of Management Science Activities

the available theoretical formulations. In revising and expanding the phases, a review of some relevant prior research was undertaken. This review contributed new concepts for phases, finer shadings of meanings, and some ideas about variables which could be used to define the phases more sharply. Existing formulations that could replace the Radnor-Rubenstein model, however, were not found.

The Radnor-Rubenstein phases made the histories of management science activities conceptually manageable, and they have suggested many research questions to Radnor and his colleagues.[13] In addition, the idea of phases promised an opportunity to develop temporal parameters. Although it was unclear which phases might be defined, some kind of distinct phases appeared to be an appropriate descriptive device for the data collected through the spring of 1968. The concept of phases offered the opportunity of an operational description, while the abandonment of phases left the research with no direction. For these reasons the concept of phases was retained in the search for a more adequate descriptive model of the development of management science activities.

The second basic idea for a new descriptive model is that of mutual accommodation. (In the next section this idea will be developed at length.) A preliminary examination of the Radnor-Rubenstein five-phase model suggests, first, that there was a need for a more adequate model to encompass what seemed to be two alternative patterns of development for management science activities; second, that the notion of a description involving phases could be retained, and third, that there was a need for grounding any new model in theoretical concepts taken from organizational research.

Mutual Accommodation

Several researchers have been concerned with the mutual accommodation between the members of organizational units and those of the larger organization. Especially relevant here are writers who have studied the development of new staff activities or staff functions which, like management science functions, are composed of research professionals with the mission of creating and introducing changes based on technological specializations.[14] In this section, studies of mutual accommodation between organizations and their research, or planning, units will be reviewed. The review suggests the variables and concepts that will be used in a new descriptive phase model.

Early in his study of scientists in industry, William Kornhauser proposes that mutual accommodation occurs between researchers and their host organizations, that "professional work requires considerable independence, but complex organizations require coordination of professional work with other functions of the total enterprise. It is processes of mutual accommodation that result, both professions and organizations are modified."[15] Organizations accommodate by allowing the scientist to organize his work in a familiar, unstructured manner and by allowing him to pursue professional activities and be judged according to scientific criteria. Professionals, in turn, adapt to organizational demands: "by conforming to industrial routines; accepting the responsibility for seeking commercially feasible devices; frequently assuming administrative positions; working closely with operations; and so on."[16]

In an article on long-range planners, John Berry, rather than emphasizing the necessity of accommodation, chooses to note its existence in a passage which illustrates the organization man's awareness of mutual accommodation:

With the passage of time, companies and planners have had to revise some of their original ideas about their mutual relationship. Three years ago *Time* magazine quoted Booz, Allen and Hamilton consultant John P. Gallagher as saying, "Ideally, the corporate planner would have a law degree, an engineering degree, and be able to walk on water." By now, though, industry seems to have given up hope of finding such supermen.

The planners, for their part, seem to be trying harder than ever to keep their feet on the ground. The National Society for Corporate Planning adopted "Pragmatic Planning" as last year's theme, and most recent articles stress the down-to-earth approach.

Does this growing mutual accommodation perhaps point to a greater job longevity for the planner?[17]

This passage indicates some variables that may be dimensions of accommodation: expectations of the organization regarding the magnitude and utility of the changes to be introduced; departure from conventional procedures (daring innovativeness) of the new staff activity; and divergence of the staff's work and the organization's concerns.

Burns and Stalker are also concerned with adaptation, particularly with that of the organization to new structures of relations between people in order to effectively use research and development activities. Much of their book is devoted to a discussion of why the organizations they studied did not make the necessary adaptations, but several cases of successful (within their theory) adaptation are noted.[18] Particularly relevant here is that Burns and Stalker are concerned with adaptation, not in the sense of each side giving in a bit on some desire—not compromise—but an adaptation in the sense that something new, a new form of organization, emerges from mutual adaptation. Mutual accommodation, then, need not be a process of "splitting the difference" between antagonistic sides, to use the terminology of Haas. Accommodation may involve what Haas calls "upgrading the conflict to a higher level."[19]

Robert Avery writes of the "enculturation" of the new researcher into an industrial R&D laboratory in a way that is suggestive for the management science specialist:

Enculturation seems an apt term to refer to the social process whereby the young technical man becomes transformed, or transforms himself, into an established industrial researcher. As he begins his career, he is not merely confronted with technical problems awaiting solution. He must define and solve these problems in ways which are appropriate to the culture of the industrial laboratory. Part of his task, then, is to learn a new culture.[20]

The culture the researcher learns is not constant, Avery notes, for "it is in the industrial laboratory that the two worlds, science and business, meet and work out their mutual accommodations."[21] The enculturation of the researcher involves learning how to sell his ideas within the organization, for within the organizational context, "ideas lack validity until he can secure approval to test and use them."[22] Selling ideas involves learning the history of the laboratory and its projects, the constraints on the lab and other units of the organization, and the economics and social relations necessary to be an effective "salesman." Avery recognizes that some researchers are not willing to make the accommodations necessary to present their ideas effectively to managers who are uninvolved and uninterested in technical detail. He also emphasizes the trial-and-error nature of this enculturation process.[23]

It seems unnecessary to specify the kind of research this process may involve. Avery argues for the rejection of pure versus applied distinctions while noting that in an organizational context all researchers may be constrained to direct their thinking toward ideas that may be of benefit to the company or at least to consider how these ideas may be applied in the company. Similarly, management science specialists face the problem of relating their technical competence to their organization if they are to be useful to the organization. Group leaders sometimes have their staffs undertake special projects designed either to increase their competence in a technique relevant to the organization or to increase their knowledge of the organization's operations.

Through over 100 interviews, Avery demonstrated that enculturation—or accommodation by the researcher—does exist. He outlines the process by which a technical specialist becomes a useful member of the organization. He concentrates, however, on researchers who are just assuming their first job. This emphasis is not necessary, for all researchers find it necessary to become familiar with the organization employing them whenever they take a new job. For successive jobs the learning process is perhaps easier, in that a researcher usually has developed ways to learn how to learn.

In a study of 10 organizations with R&D laboratories, Kornhauser finds many ways in which an organization accommodates to the scientists in its midst, as well as ways in which it adapts the scientists themselves. One way to obtain accommodation on the part of the research staff is by design, by using recruitment criteria. Some organizations recruit their scientists with varying attention to the recruit's organizational skills:

Those that emphasize professional criteria (such as research originality, technical skills, and the like) naturally tend to recruit more from universities, to look for men with advanced degrees, and to use their own scientists for recruitment, whereas those that stress organizational criteria (such as interest in the company, capacity to work with others, leadership skills, and the like) tend to recruit more from other companies, to look for men with industrial experience, and to rely primarily on management judgment in recruitment.[24]

This is not to say that organizational and technical skills are incompatible.[25] The internal organization of the laboratory is another way in which researchers evidence adaptation to an organization, Kornhauser notes, with specialist groupings being more consistent with professional orientations and task groupings with organizational orientations.[26] Control over publication is a device management can use to adapt a research group to an organization (with those oriented toward professional publication being either indulged or deprived, depending on the need.[27] Control over project selection is another.[28] Work evaluation is still another means of accommodation. Perhaps a scientist's work is judged by several people—among the professional group, by specialists or task leaders, or on a wider basis, by professionals or "organizationals," with the two types here reflecting a decreasing accommodation of professional norms.[29]

Kornhauser notes that a major influence on the degree to which the accommodation is in favor of the professionals is the extent to which the organization is dependent on their professional work. "The greater the organization's dependence on basic science for its objectives, the greater likelihood that it will adapt to the demands of the scientists that they be allowed major responsibility to select research problems, determine research strategy, and communicate results."[30] Another accommodation the organization may make with its scientists is to allow them to pursue professional status. Because of the combinations of time and money that are possible, this is a continuous variable. An organization may allow time off for professional meetings, to present papers or otherwise. It may pay for the time and expense involved. Additionally, there are several plans for encouraging a researcher to further his professional training.[31] Promotion of researchers to management positions is another way in which an organization may attempt to adapt to the research activity, feeling that researchers-turned-administrators will better understand the research group.[32] This, Kornhauser notes, may also be an attempt to control researchers when an organization tries to transform professional matters into administrative ones.[33] Another way in which an organization attempts to accommodate to the scientists is to develop multiple career ladders in which research autonomy, remuneration, and freedom from administrative duties are one set of rewards and administrative responsibility, remuneration, and promotion out of the laboratory are another.

In sum, Kornhauser finds a wide variety of ways in which an organization may accommodate its professional researchers. Many may be used to shape a research group, to influence its accommodations as a group, over a period of time, although this is not Kornhauser's perspective explicitly. A case study by Todd La Porte which admittedly involves an uncommon situation confirms many of the types of accommodation discussed by Kornhauser.[34] Unlike Burns and Stalker, Kornhauser's dimensions, or variables, are related to what one usually thinks of as the desires of professional researchers. While they are controlled by the organization, these variables generally describe the behavior permitted the researcher, rather than any ongoing features of the clients of the research group.

Kornhauser gives some indication that the accommodation process need not be the same at all times, although basically he is concerned with established laboratories rather than new ones. For example, he notes that initially research is not well understood, that it "needs protection from well-established units" to allow it to develop "inner strength and a capacity for self-defense." Only then "can it be brought into close working relations with other departments in order that it can make a maximum contribution to company goals."[35]

As we have seen, Kornhauser's, Avery's, and LaPorte's studies of research and development laboratories in the United States, Burns' and Stalker's study of research and development in Great Britain, and Berry's essay about American, corporate, long-range planners all describe the mutual accommodation of researchers and research groups with managers and the organization. Management science activities are internal research and analysis functions which are similar to scientific research or planning functions in terms of member professionalism, the activity's science or technology base, and the purpose of innovation. From this review of the literature, it appears that the concept of mutual accommodation can be a useful guide for a new descriptive model of the development of management science activities.

Variables for Describing the Mutual Accommodation of a Management Science Activity and Its Host Agency

The idea of mutual accommodation raises the question of selecting variables which indicate aspects of that accommodation and which also might help in defining the phases. Five variables will be proposed in this section. One will come from considering the ideas of accommodation and phases together. Three will come from contrasting evolutionary and revolutionary patterns, and one will come from the idea of accommodation directly.

These five variables describe salient features of the management science activity, its host agency, and the relations between the two. Together they provide a basis for describing the state of a management science activity at any given time.

The Phases of Accommodation

Two studies of organizational change suggest that change is accepted by organizations in phases. These studies use terms for those phases which do not reflect the nature of management science activities as agents of change, or as innovations. The concept of *legitimacy,* which is an alternative, is the first variable.

A new management science activity can be viewed as a *change agent* acting on an organization or as an innovation to be adopted or rejected by the organization. The work of Edgar Schein and Warren Bennis on personal change is relevant to the former perspective; that of Everett Rogers on the adoption of innovations concerns the latter. Both use simple phase models to discuss the process of change.

In discussing the process of change in laboratory training, Schein and Bennis propose three phases—unfreezing, change, and refreezing: "Unfreezing readies a person to pay attention to new categories of information about himself as a prelude to redefining his assumptions, beliefs, and constructs about himself and his relationships to others."[36] Whether someone is "unfrozen" depends on his motivation to learn, the existence of a situation of disconfirmation of accepted beliefs, an induction of anxiety or guilt, and a reduction of threat.[37] When a person begins to "thaw," he moves into the phase of *changing*. In this period he either looks about him for new cues or seeks out someone with whom he can identify.

Once a person begins to acquire new beliefs, perspectives, and points of view, his attitudes and behavioral responses begin to change. Whether or not these changes remain stable depends, however, upon the degree to which they fit into the rest of the personality (personal refreezing) or are reinforced and confirmed by important others with whom the person has a relationship (relational refreezing).[38]

In this phase of refreezing, the new beliefs and orientations become a more permanent part of the person who has changed. Although Schein and Bennis do not say this, it would seem that in refreezing, the new orientations are elaborated and reconciled or rationalized with other parts of the person's belief system. The behavioral implications of the new orientations are tested, and new behaviors become routinized. The introduction of management science into an agency can be conceptualized in similar terms, although Schein and Bennis emphasize that *"effective unfreezing is not possible in most organizations."*[39]

The early life of a management science activity may involve attempts by its members to "unfreeze" unreceptive managers. In this period the staff analysts may seek, through various actions and statements, to obtain for their ideas and approaches an openminded hearing and possibly, authorization to begin projects. As this phase develops it is succeeded by a *change* phase, in which researcher and manager begin to attempt new patterns of behavior—joint work on management science projects, new approaches to problem definition, and so on. Then, if these new behaviors are thought to be personally rewarding or are rewarded by the organization, the behaviors become more routine and the organizational patterns are "refrozen."

Basic ideas from studies of the diffusion of innovations suggest an alternative formulation of phases. Everett Rogers views the adoption of innovations as a process of distinct stages and cites research empirically confirming his stages.[40] The stages he proposes are awareness, interest, evaluation, trial and adoption.[41] Contrasting Rogers' view with Schein's and Bennis's suggests the following:

Rogers	Schein and Bennis
awareness interest evaluation	unfreezing
trial	changing
adoption	refreezing

Awareness, interest, and evaluation all are processes which have as their outcome the trial of an innovation. In management science, adopting managers can be influenced by researchers and the change-agent mission of the staff, as well as by the technology. Consequently, awareness and evaluation may occur close together. Before a "trial" is likely, a manager may have to be "unfrozen" about the personal and change-agent aspects of the management science activity.

The complexity of management science as an innovation makes both the Rogers and the Schein and Bennis terminology inadequate. Schein and Bennis make no reference to the nature of the change agent; they refer only to relationships within those affected by the innovation. Rogers refers to the change being considered, but his work mentions only discrete changes. Needed are terms which capture the idea that management science involves people and technology combined into a mission of generating change. Furthermore, the terms desired should be oriented toward the innovation, rather than merely indicating the properties of the adopters.

The term *legitimacy* captures both the continuous and the discrete nature of management science as an innovation. It implies an orientation toward the innovation. Rogers and Schein and Bennis imply that accommodation to innovations is at least a two-step process involving agreeing to a trial and confirming an adoption. Together, legitimacy and accommodation to innovation in two steps yield the following labels for phases. These labels are compared with Rogers and Schein and Bennis in Table 2-1. Legitimacy, then, is the first of the five variables describing the state of a management science activity.

Other Accommodation Variables

In this section we will look at the technical competence of manage-

Table 2-1
Three Phases of Legitimacy for a Management Science Activity.

This Study	Schein and Bennis	Rogers
No legitimacy for the management science activity in the agency or attempt to gain tentative legitimacy	unfreezing	awareness interest evaluation
Managment science activity has tentative legitimacy or attempt to consolidate tentative legitimacy	change	trial
Management science activity is routinely accepted as a legitimate function and group in the agency	refreezing	adoption

ment scientists as an important descriptive variable. Management scientists are a possible barrier to accommodation. For example, an agency with little experience in dealing with management science technology may hire a staff of highly skilled management scientists. This may lead to friction between the management scientists, who want to perform studies commensurate with their skills, and the managers, who cannot understand the studies. Conversely, the accommodation process may be slowed if the management scientists lack the skills to keep pace with the rate of innovation an agency can accept. The technical competence of the management scientists is also an important feature of a management science activity, in that it affects the nature and number of studies completed, as well as the mutual accommodation process.

The second of the five variables is the *skills level* of the management scientists, with *skills* referring to technical, management science ability.

Three other aspects of management science activities can be obtained by contrasting the evolutionary and revolutionary patterns suggested in the preliminary examination of the Radnor-Rubenstein phases: *technology, innovativeness,* and *aggressiveness*. Three variables stand out in an examination of the differences between management science activities in each of these two patterns. First, those in a revolutionary pattern appear to be very *aggressive* toward the host agency. *Missionary* is a term that is often used by management scientists. In contrast, the orientation toward the host agency of management science activities in an evolutionary pattern is better described by the term *passive*. Second, those activities in a revolutionary pattern appear to send many more recommendations for change to their host agencies than do those of an evolutionary pattern. This might be called *innovativeness* if that term does not imply an evaluation of the recommendations. Third, the activities of a revolutionary pattern claim both the competence and the desire to do technically advanced management science studies, while the activities of an evolutionary pattern appear to be much more modest about their competence and desires regarding the *level of technology*.

Along with skills level and legitimacy, the variables, aggressiveness, innovativeness, and level of technology comprise the five variables for describing the development of a management science activity. Each indexes a different aspect of mutual accommodation. Legitimacy suggests a time dimension in addition to the orientation of the agency. Skills level suggests a barrier to accommodation. Aggressiveness, innovativeness, and level of technology combined suggest two different styles of accommodation.

3

A Revised Model of the Development of Management Science Activities in Government Agencies

In Chapter 2 we saw five variables for the description of the mutual accomodation of a management science activity and its host agency. In this chapter these variables become the basis of a many-phased model of the development of management science activities.

Definition of Five Variables

The First Variable

The first variable is the *skills level* of the management science activity. This refers specifically to formal training and work experience in operations research, systems analysis, management science, and closely related disciplines. Skills level is divided into three values—high, medium, and low. *High* generally refers to a person with a Ph.D. in a management science discipline or someone with a master's degree and perhaps five or more years' experience practicing management science. *Medium* skills level refers to a person with a recent master's degree or its equivalent in training and experience in management science. *Low* skills level refers to a recent graduate of an MBA or MPA program who has a couple of statistics courses, or perhaps to an experienced government staff person who has taken some short seminars in analytical methods and is familiar with the systems approach, or again perhaps, to an administrator who has an engineering background but whose quantitative skills have become not unrecoverably rusty. Skills level, then, refers specifically to skills in quantitative analysis and formal modeling. Experienced administrators, of course, have other important skills which are not at issue here.

The Second Variable

The second variable is the *level of technology* used by the management science activity. This is a combination of the technical complexity and the social scope of the management science projects undertaken by the activity. By *technical complexity* I mean the degree of difficulty of the technical problems encountered, the novelty of the specific methods used, and the variety of methods used on a project—all judged in the context of the time at which the project is conducted. By *social scope* I mean the sheer size of the project in terms of the number of people involved in it, the complexity of the division of labor, the time pressures that may strain the project's social system, and the number of managers who, without working directly on the project, must cooperate with those who are. At first glance, this second aspect of level of technology may seem out of place, but I feel that management science projects are social, not just technical, systems and that the application of the technology is made more difficult in socially complex projects. Therefore, one of the technical skills of the management science project's leader is the application of management science in organizational settings. This social side of technology is secondary to the purely technical side. However, here it is assumed there is a trade-off between the two in determining the level of technology used by the management science activity. A technically esoteric, but socially simple, project may be considered equivalent to a somewhat less esoteric, but organizationally involved, one.

There are three levels of technology: high level, low level, and prior. *High level* refers to projects which require major inputs from highly skilled management science analysts or which can be conducted by analysts with medium-level technical skills but which are socially complex. *Low level* refers to projects which can be conducted by analysts with medium-level skills and which are not very complex socially or which require only minor inputs from such analysts but which are socially complex. *Prior* technology refers to projects which, however complex socially, require no input from analysts with medium-level management science skills.

Figure 3-1 shows these three levels of technology in a two-dimensional space of required skills level and social complexity. The pictorial representation is designed to illustrate the trade-offs be-

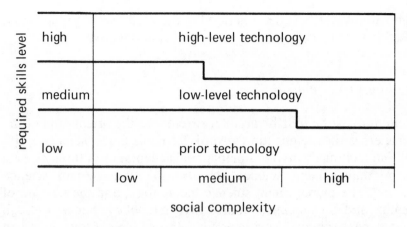

Figure 3-1. Pictorial Representation of Trade-Offs between Required Skills Level and Social Complexity in the Determination of Level of Technology

tween the two components of level of technology, but it should not be considered definitive.

The Third Variable

The third variable is *innovativeness*, which refers to the number of change recommendations sent from the activity to the organization. These recommendations include those based on management science projects or concepts. Innovativeness is divided into three levels—highly, moderately, and slightly innovative. Highly innovative management science activities are regularly used as advisors and produce serious project recommendations every four to six weeks. Moderately innovative management science activities produce serious project recommendations three to six times a year and do some advising as well. Slightly innovative activities produce project recommendations only occasionally and are not often used as advisors.

To some extent, these definitions must be qualified by the size of the management science group, especially at the large end. That is, very large management science activities might be considered only moderately innovative if they produce major change recommendations no more often than groups half the size, which are considered highly innovative. At the other end of the scale, small groups may, by their very size, be unable to be highly innovative.

The Fourth Variable

Legitimacy is the fourth variable. It refers to the orientation of the managers in the organization toward the management science activity. Full legitimacy involves managerial acceptance of three aspects of the management science activity: the management science analysts, the management science technology, and the mission of creating and introducing administrative and policy changes through management science. Legitimacy has three levels. First, there can be no legitimacy for the management science activity. Second, there can be tentative legitimacy when the activity has been tentatively accepted, subject to later assessment of its performance. Third, there is full legitimacy when the activity's performance and behavior have been found acceptable and the orientation of clients and other managers moves from one of doubting that the activity can produce useful outputs in an acceptable manner to one of assuming that there will be good reason if it does not.

The Fifth Variable

Aggressiveness is the fifth and last variable. It refers to the orientation of the activity toward the host organization. At one extreme is the "missionary" activity, the activity that aggressively sells itself and its technology to potential clients. This may involve making un- solicited proposals; undertaking studies without a client, in anticipa- tion of later selling the results; making extravagant claims about what management science can accomplish; and so on. At the other extreme is the "passive" activity which undertakes little or no management science work unless the client comes to it first with a specific request and a clearly defined issue. Such an activity makes few claims or promises. Finally, there is the "routine" activity which sometimes responds to client requests by retaining substan- tial freedom to redefine the issues presented and which may also pursue a promising project on its own. The important distinction is not that the routine activity may be passive or missionary but that it is neither. Instead, social relations between the activity and its clients have evolved to the point where the distinction between aggressive and passive is not an issue. The activity will be passive with some clients, aggressive with others, depending on what seems appropriate to the indiviudual client and moment.

These five variables and their three values are summarized in Table 3-1. Many configurations of the five variables and their values are possible, and a subset of them is empirically likely.

Variables and Phases

My purpose in defining these variables is to be able to use them to define the phases of the model of management science development. The five variables are shown in Table 3-2.

While Table 3-2 names phases and defines them in terms of the values of the five variables, the configuration of variables into phases is not self-evident. The ideas underlying most of the phases already existed in my mind before the five variables were articulated and defined. In the actual research process I used the five variables to refine my ideas about the phases that had arisen out of field experience and attempts to revise the Radnor-Rubenstein model. These ideas were connected to the variable definitions through an elaborate process of arranging and rearranging cards on which were written all possible configurations of the five variables (there were 243 configurations). Some configurations made no sense, while others seemed roughly equivalent. Overall, the variable configurations yielded twelve phases and these are named in the left column of Table 3-2. In this section these phases will be discussed in a narrative manner and ambiguities in the definitions treated. The phase names are chosen for descriptive purposes.

Table 3-1
Five Variables and the Three Values for Each

Legitimacy	none	tentative	consolidated
Aggressiveness	aggressive, missionary	Passive	Routinized relations
Innovativeness	slightly	moderately	highly
Skills	low	medium	high
Technology	prior	low-level	high-level

Table 3-2
Twelve Phases in the Development of Management Science and Their Definitions in Terms of Five Trichotomized Variables

Phases	Skills	Technology	Variables Innovativeness	Legitimacy	Aggressiveness
GAINING TENTATIVE LEGITIMACY— EVOLUTIONARY (development of organizational role and discovery of problems)	low, medium, high	prior or low-level	slightly to moderately	none	passive
GAINING TENTATIVE LEGITIMACY— REVOLUTIONARY (missionary exposure)	low, medium, or high	prior or low-level	slightly	none	aggressive
(missionary application)	high or medium	high-level or low-level	slightly or moderately	none	aggressive
(missionary application and exposure)	high or medium	high-level or low-level	highly or moderately	none	aggressive
CONSOLIDATING LEGITIMACY— EVOLUTIONARY (gradual consolidation)	high, medium, or low	low-level	moderately or slightly	tentative	passive
CONSOLIDATING LEGITIMACY— REVOLUTIONARY (rapid consolidation)	high or medium	high-level or low-level	moderately to highly	tentative	aggressive

ROUTINIZED CHANGE AGENT ROLE (prior technology)	low, medium	prior	slightly	none, most likely, but possibly tentative or consolidated	routinized
(low-level management science technology)	medium or high	low-level	moderately or highly	consolidated	routinized
(high-level management science technology)	high	high-level	highly or moderately	consolidated	routinized
PROCESSING ROLE (prior technology)	low, medium or high	prior	slightly	none; possibly tentative	passive
(low-level technology)	medium or high	low-level	slightly	none, or tentative or high	passive
(high-level technology)	high or medium	high-level	slightly	none or tentative or high	passive

*Gaining Tentative Legitimacy: Evolutionary and
Revolutionary*

In the evolutionary phase an activity passively uses, at best, a low
level of management science technology regardless of the activity's
capability, and it produces few innovations. Here the activity has no
legitimacy and does not seek legitimacy aggressively in terms of the
technology used, the recommendations sent out, the claims made,
or the social relations pursued.

In the revolutionary phase, which has three subphases, the opposite occurs. Legitimacy is sought aggressively. *Missionary exposure* refers to a situation in which legitimacy is sought through
aggressive "selling" and social interaction. *Missionary application*
refers to a situation in which legitimacy is sought through the application of a level of technology well beyond the ability of the client (if
there is one) to understand, and recommendations are produced of a
type and volume that are well beyond the current level of interest in
the organization. Sometimes the two may occur simultaneously in a
phase of *missionary application and exposure* when the organization is exposed to a barrage on all possible fronts which is aimed at
getting it to accept the management science activity. According to
Table 3-2, it may not be possible to distinguish this subphase from
the previous one. The distinguishing feature of missionary application *and* exposure from missionary application is the amount of
active communication about the glories of management science that
occurs, in addition to the application of advanced management
science technology without the support of an informed client.

*Consolidating Legitimacy: Evolutionary and
Revolutionary*

These two phases are analogous to a trial period in which the number
of managers sufficient to assure the activity's short-run future have
become clients of the management science activity. According to
the idea behind this phase, their commitment to the activity is still
dependent on the results of the activity's work. The activity in this
phase can be passive or aggressive toward its clients, in terms of the
level of technology used and the amount of innovation produced, as
well as social and communications relations. In the *evolutionary*

subphase, in which the technology used is not advanced, consultants may be used to bolster the activity's skills level.

The Routinized Change Agent Role

The phase *routinized change agent role* is intended to emphasize that in this phase the management science activity is not only accepted but is accepted as a source of change. In a wider context one reason for being concerned with management science in government or business is that management science may be an example of an attempt by organizational leaders to adapt to a more complex and competitive world through internal development of change- generating functions.

Routinized change is the focus in this general phase. The technology underlying the change role is divided into three parts which correspond to three subphases. The first involves routinized change but without management science technology being used. To one interested in the use of management science, two more desirable subphases can be distinguished here. They are based on the use of either low-level or high-level management science technology.

The Processing Role

There is one other general phase in Figure 3-2 which is called the *processing role*. It describes a state that is observed empirically as well as one that is a theoretical possibility. Here we have a situation in which a management science activity has completed one or more large projects which lead not to a one-time recommendation but usually to a computerized model designed to be rerun to produce recommendations for a regularly recurring issue. One example is a model that is used to calculate debt placement and retirement. Another is a model for selecting ways of disposing periodically of surplus commodities. Once a model like this is operational, it may be run periodically and even updated slightly. In the *processing role* phase this is all that is done; no new projects are undertaken. Instead, a staff probably smaller than that which constructed and tested the model remains to run it. This phase, then, represents a state in which an old management science model is still producing

34

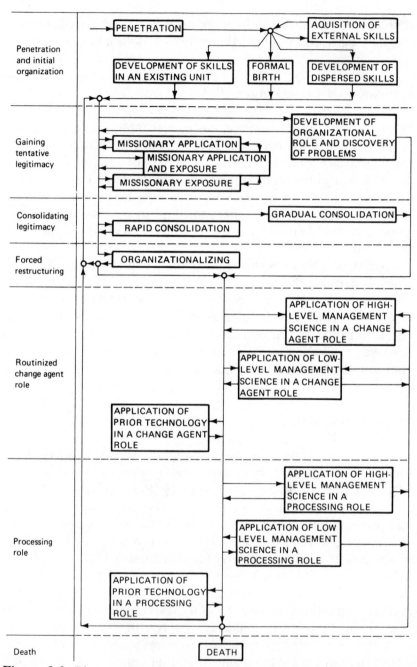

Figure 3-2. Pictorial Representation of the Descriptive Phase Model of the Development of Management Science Activities

useful recommendations, but it is a state in which no new work is actually being done. Instead, old work is being *processed* again. The model being processed can be based on the three different levels of technology shown in Table 3-1.

The major way such a phase can be distinguished from others which may appear similar in Table 3-2 is through the coder's knowledge of the activity's history as it is revealed in the available data. The processing role phase implies details about prior project work which are normally verifiable.

Pictorial Representation of the Model

We are now at the point at which a pictorial representation of the entire phase model can be given. It is important to move from Table 3-2 to the pictorial representation of Figure 3-2 because, in the latter figure, one can see that no linear development is assumed. A management science activity can move up or down through the phases listed vertically in Table 3-2. In addition, there are several residual phases to be discussed.

The major phases of the phase model of management science have been discussed and defined through narrative and tabular presentation. So far, nothing has been said about progress through these phases. Except for some small details, Table 3-2 is an algorithm for translating codings of the five variables into specific phases. If the management science activities can be coded according to these five variables, the activities can be coded into phases. (The results of the coding are used in Chapter 5.) This section of Chapter 3 has shown how the variables can be translated into phases.

Further Details of the Phase Model

As can be seen by comparing Table 3-2 and Figure 3-2, three phases remain to be presented. These are *death, forced restructuring*, and *penetration and initial organization*. Management science activities have a beginning, however gradual or surreptitious. Management science analysts sometimes tell stories about "bootleg" management science activities in which management science technology is used without higher managers being told. Or the activity may have a formal mission statement and job descriptions and be announced in the "house organ". Whatever the form, there is a need for a name for these beginnings, which are given at the top of Figure 3-2. Management science activities may also be terminated. Radnor and Rubenstein called this "death", a name I have retained here.

Phases for Beginnings and Ends

The *death* phase refers to a state in which the management science activity disappears as an organizational unit. The following are *not* death: reorganization, absorption into a larger unit, temporary loss of management science skills, relocation, major personnel changeover, and substantial loss of accrued legitimacy. The following situations *are* death: the management science group is disbanded as an organizational unit and its staff dispersed; the management science activity stops doing management science work and ceases being a source of change, and if it ever does undertake management science work again does so only with the addition of new staff, sponsorship, and mission statement; the management science group is disbanded, and even though another management science activity is initiated shortly thereafter elsewhere in the organization, it has a different staff, different clientele, and probably different sponsorship; and, the management science activity is disbanded, but other management science activities in the same organization continue independently without substantial change in mission, domain, or personnel.

Penetration and initial organization denotes the fact that before a management science group is formally established, there may be a period in which establishment is considered. It is comparable to the Radnor-Rubenstein phases, *prebirth* and *birth*. Further, management science groups may begin in a number of ways. One is for a new unit to be chartered to do management science. Another is for management science analysts to be hired into or trained from and returned to an existing organizational unit, or for mathematically trained people in an existing unit to begin doing management science. Still another is for people with some management science skills who are located in different parts of the organization to be formed into a loose group, each member of which spends some time working on management-science-related matters. Before or concurrently with each of these three forms of organization, the management of the host organization may hire consultants to help in the initiation of the activity. Determining the beginning of a period of penetration is impossible; there is no way of discovering just who in an organization first became acquainted with management science and when. What can be done, though, is to note a time at which the beginnings of penetration are obvious. The three different forms of management science organization are important partly because changes in the form of organization may indicate important changes in phase.

One Phase Derived from Field Experience

There is a final phase in the model which cannot be derived from the five-variable scheme and which has not been noted in any of the research literature on organizational change, innovation, or management science that I know of. Events similar to those presented in the description of this phase seem to have stimulated concern in research on management science since A.H. Rubenstein's initial article in 1960.[1] However, these events have never been articulated as a distinct phase in a process of change or development.

This phase has been observed in a number of cases in the field, and each time it exhibits similar features. In this subsection these common features will be stated and interpreted. This speculation is attempted partly because it helps identify the phase for coding. Other phases derivable from the five-variable scheme need coding only on these variables. This phase is not as precisely defined; therefore, a more interpretive presentation is given. The phase is *forced restructuring* or *organizationalizing*.

Management science activities may experience sudden and drastic changes. I have followed several management science activities through such changes, and those I have observed have at least the following characteristics in common: (1) they occur in a short period of time, say, about six weeks; (2) substantial staff losses occur through resignation or dismissal, not all of which are necessarily replaced; (3) there is a change in the projects undertaken, with some projects either being discontinued or modified substantially. In addition, the following characteristics may be present: (4) the locus of initiation of projects moves out of the management science activity and into the hands of clients or supervisors of the management science activity; (5) the level of technology and the skills level in the activity decline; (6) the activity becomes less missionary; (7) the activity's legitimacy seems to change sharply; (8) the characteristics of project work change toward simpler and shorter-term projects.

In the cases observed, one possible interpretation of these changes stood out. The changes seemed to be in directions that make the management science activity more comprehensible to managers and more controlled by them. Further, these periods did not just happen; they were the consequence of actions taken by higher managers, and these actions were opposed by some management science analysts. Therefore, these periods are called *forced restructuring*, a term which indicates that the management science activity is being redesigned against the will of its current leadership.

Forced restructuring, as it has been described here, might also be called *organizationalizing*, a term intended to imply that the management science activity is being changed to something more like the rest of the organization and more responsive to the rest of the organization. It appears to be, then, a period during which conscious design decisions, perhaps previously neglected, are being made for management science activity. It is a period in which the support of individual managers for one or another concept of a management science activity is in flux. It is a risky period, the consequence of which may be permanent loss of management science skills from the activity or even the death of the activity.

The description of this phase has been more interpretive than that of other phases because it is not anticipated analytically. Instead, it has been discovered in and described from field experience. If it is a meaningful category, other observers should be able to recognize and code it on the basis of the description given here.

Figure 3-2 presents the phases defined through the five-variable scheme in the previous section of this chapter. In addition, this representation of the phase model includes three other general phases and their varieties, which are described in this section. Two of the phases serve to mark beginnings and ends of the organizational life of a management science activity. The third phase results from field experience; a particular pattern and sequence of behavior, which has been observed in the field several times, has been named, described and interpreted.

This completes the listing and description of the phases. The descriptions of the phases have been rooted as closely as possible in the five variables. With the variables and phases described, the last task in this chapter is to indicate temporal relations among phases.

An Illustrative Trip Through the Phase Model

There are many possible routes through the phase model. Figure 3-2 is not meant to imply that a top-to-bottom progression is necessary. The lines linking the phases go up and down, left and right, and no value is imputed to any direction of movement. In Figure 3-3 a hypothetical trip through the phases is presented. This "trip" gives an idea of the variety of ways in which management science activity might develop. It also indicates the possible complexity of development. The trip will be more elaborate than the usual ones. (Actual development patterns will be discussed in Chapter 5.) In Figures 3-2 and 3-3, the phases are connected by lines, so that there is at least one path between any two phases such that no other phase must be traversed en route. I concede that I have found no simple way to draw these paths.

Enter the model at *penetration* (1)[a]. From there, a group is organized as part of an existing staff, (*development of skills in an existing unit*) (2). The staff begins performing esoteric management science studies which clients do not understand or, necessarily, do not really want, but no attempt is made to proselytize on behalf of management science (*missionary application*) (3). Eventually managers come to view the management science staff as deficient, and they arrange for the firing of the group leader. When the group leader leaves, most of the management science work stops, and the group is in a disorganized and confused state for several months (*organizationalizing*) (4). A new group leader is chosen, this time an experienced staff person from the organization. But the most skilled management science analysts have left the group, and potential clients feel that they have been burned by their past experience with management science and therefore do not feel that it will be relevant to them. The reconstituted group thus starts without much in the way of legitimacy. The new leader then realizes that he must move very slowly. He avoids any missionary activity (*development of organizational role and discovery of problems*) (5). Eventually he

---

[a]Numbers refer to the path lines in Figure 3-3.

manages to get several clients interested in some fairly simple projects. Upon successful completion of these projects, a number of clients change their views of management science, and the new leader is allowed to hire a highly skilled management scientist for a particular project for which the group's skills are not adequate. With these actions the group moves into a phase of (*gradual consolidation of tentative legitimacy*) (6). The group continues to perform in ways that are well received by several important clients. After a year or so the group leader retires, and there is considerable debate about what kind of new leader should be hired. Finally another highly experienced management science analyst is hired and the group moves perceptibly into the (*routinized change agent role*) phase (7). But most of the work the group does is still straightforward management science. The projects are management science projects, but they are not technically advanced nor very large in scope. This is (*application of low-level management science in a change agent role*) (7). As the years pass, the group undertakes several major projects each of which involves several man-years of professional effort, as well as the skills commonly held only by Ph.D. analysts. The group has moved into (*application of high-level management science in a change agent role*) (8). While in this phase, there is a major management shake-up, and the new top management is initially hostile to management science. They do not allow new projects to begin, and the group continues to operate several old models for its clients (*processing high level management science*) (9). After about six months, however, the new management allows the management science group to pick up on new projects, and the group returns to the (*application of high-level management science in a change agent role*) (10).

This hypothetical trip through the phases illustrates how the phase model represented in Figures 3-2 and 3-3 can be used to trace the development of management science activity over a period of time. The phase model allows a dynamic progression through time, as well as a variety of complicated phase sequences. Other phase models of adoption, such as Rogers' five-phase model for technical innovations, assume only one possible sequence of phases, a sequence that may or may not be completed. The relative complexity of the phase model presented here, to describe the development of management science as a complicated sociotechnical innovation, may reflect a corresponding complexity of that development and adoption process.

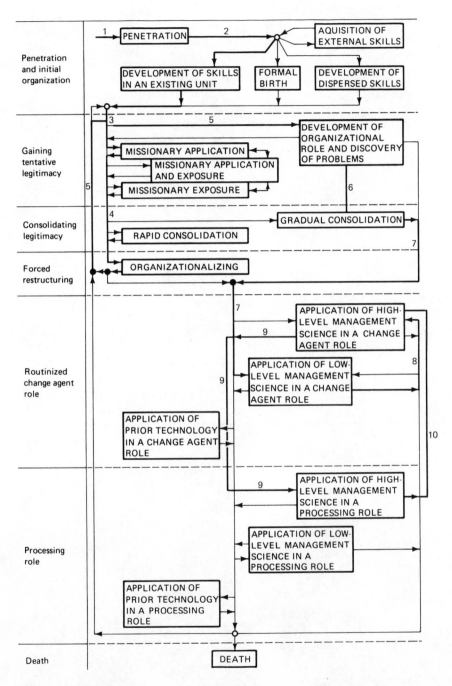

Figure 3-3. Pictorial Representation of the Descriptive Phase
Model, with an Illustration of a Complex Path

4

Field Methods and Coding

Exploratory research requires a diversity of methods. In seeking a pattern in complex experiences, false starts must be expected and multiple perspectives sought, even at the cost of seeming to be disorderly. Not all potential management science activities were judged actual ones; some were richer sources of insights than others. Accordingly some groups were studied more intensively than others. Research began with semistructured interviews. Based on these, structured instruments were prepared and used both in interviews and as questionnaires. The resulting extensive data base of 1,100 pages of interview transcripts and 1,500 pages of questionnaires posed a challenging coding task which was resolved through carefully defining the phases in terms of variables (see Chapter 3) more immediately observable in the raw data and through the careful training of a coder.

While both field methods and coding are extensively documented elsewhere, the essential operations used to produce the data are presented in this chapter. When the coding technique is combined with this data, the result is a method of formalizing the richness of case study materials into more systematic and testable models.

The Sample

In the course of my research, forty-six groups in thirty-seven federal civilian agencies were identified as possible management science activities and were contacted one or more times.[1] David A. Tansik, of the University of Arizona, was the principal colleague for the fieldwork in this study. Harold Welsch, of Northwestern University, also conducted interviews. On occasion, I, Dr. Tansik, or Mr. Welsch was accompanied by another person. Michael Burstein assisted in the retrieval of questionnaires. In addition, contact was made with five other agencies and one special commission, in order to obtain information about federal management science from those in a position to have a government-wide perspective.

Departmental Representation

The thirty-seven agencies include executive departments, major components of executive departments, and independent agencies. Table 4-1 lists these executive departments and the distribution of groups in each. In several agencies more than one group was contacted. Of the forty-six groups, ten serve as department-wide staff. The others were either an agency within a department or an independent agency.

The Department of Defense was excluded for two reasons. One is secrecy and the other is the number, scale, and long history of management science activities in the military—two factors which make it difficult to study the development of management science activities in the Defense Department.

In addition to the thirty-seven agencies, interviews were also conducted with personnel from the Bureau of the Budget (now the Office of Management and Budget), the National Goals Research Staff, the Legislative Reference Service (now the Congressional Research Service), the Technical Analysis Division of the National Bureau of Standards, and a private firm, Westat Research.

Comparison with the Cushen survey of Washington-area operations researchers[2] and with my current knowledge suggests that this study's sample of management science activities includes well over half and possibly two-thirds of the formally organized management science activities extant in federal civilian agencies between 1967 and 1971. The sample does not include most of the management science activities outside of the Washington metropolitan area. It also does not include examples of management science activity conducted on an ad hoc basis within agencies. I have seen several examples of this in agencies employing large numbers of technically trained professionals capable of performing management science work. Finally, there are qualified management science analysts in agencies who may not be part of formally constituted management science groups and who perform little if any management science work. What I have been attempting to do here is identify formally constituted groups performing management science work, and in the

Table 4-1
Number of Agencies and Groups Contacted in Executive Departments

Department	Number of Agencies Contacted, Including Department Itself When Separate	Number of Potential Management Science Groups Contacted
Treasury	3	3
Post Office	1	1
Agriculture	4	6
Interior	4	6
Commerce	4	6
Labor	1	1
Health, Education and Welfare	8	9
Transportation	4	5
Housing and Urban Development	1	1
Independent Agencies	7	8
Total	37	46

course of this attempt such potential management science activities have been encountered.

Identification of Potential Management Science Groups

A few federal civilian agency management scientists were contacted in 1966 with the help of an acquaintance of one of the sponsors of this study. ''Snowballing'' from these existing contacts became the most frequently used method of identifying potential management science groups. Several other methods of identifying potential management science groups were used. Several management science activities were identified from the *Government Organization Manual* and the *Congressional Directory*. A small number were identified from building directories; others were identified when existing respondents changed jobs and joined or began management science activities in a different agency.

Initial contact was usually made by telephone; on several occasions, the telephone call was preceded by a letter. Letters or telephone calls stressed common points: (1) the requested interview was part of a sizable research program which had been operating in many organizations since 1960; (2) the researchers considered that field sites and respondents were participating in a *cooperative* research effort and that we anticipated maintaining relations with them for an extended period of time; (3) the respondents were promised complete confidentiality, meaning that the researchers would not identify respondents or groups directly or indirectly in print, in public conversation, or in conversations with people outside the research program. Twenty-seven of the forty-six groups were first visited in 1967. An average of five new groups was contacted in each of the next four years. Most of the activities which reported at the department level were contacted in the latter stages of the field work.

Types of Management Science Groups

Members of the groups themselves had opinions about what to call their activities and tended to use specific terms in describing their work. The largest number of groups were identified with the planning-programming-budgeting system (PPBS), but there was some distinction made between program analysis and program evaluation. Therefore analysis and evaluation have been treated as separate components of the management sciences. The next most frequent identification is with operations research. Less than half as frequently as either operations research or aspects of PPBS, respondents identified their groups with systems analysis or economic analysis (distinct from economics).

Table 4-2 presents the terms respondents used to describe their groups. While some of the groups were identified with more than one aspect of management science, this never appeared to be a source of internal conflict.

Size and Location of Management Science Tools

The forty-six groups contacted in this study differ in size, location, and reporting distance. If "small," "medium," and "large" are applied to professional staffs of one to five, six to ten, and over ten persons, respectively, most of the forty-six potential management science groups are small most of the time. Twenty-six of the groups are small throughout the period of field contact, nine are large, and five are medium. Six groups changed size categories, two of them

Table 4-2
Aspects of Management Science with Which Field Respondents Identify Their Groups

	PPBS: Policy Analysis	PPBS: Program Evaluation	Operations Research	Systems Analysis
Number of Groups Identified with This Aspect*	15	15	23	11

	Economic Analysis	Planning Systems	Benefit-Cost Analysis	Information Systems for Management
Number of Groups Identified with This Aspect*	9	5	4	2

*Most groups were identified with more than one aspect of management science by their members who were interviewed.

sharply, coincident with reorganizations and leadership changes. Other groups experienced substantial changes in the size of professional staff but not within the period of field contact.

In federal agencies management science activities appear almost exclusively in one of three functional locations: reporting directly to the agency director; within an agency's office of administration; or within an agency's office of planning and research. *Agency director* refers both to subcabinet officials with statutory authority and independent agency heads and to departmental secretaries where the groups work at the department-wide level. An "office of administration" can almost always be identified by that formal title. Planning and research offices go under a variety of names, but for our purposes, the office's title included at least one of the two terms, planning and research. Sometimes the management science activity *is* the agency's planning and research office. Twenty-seven of the forty-six groups were composed of or were part of a planning and research office; eight were part of an office of administration.

The locations of the remaining eleven varied from reporting directly to an agency director, through location in the field or program offices, to one group which floated without a formal reporting relationship.

Of the forty-six groups, the leaders of fourteen of them reported directly to the agency director. Twenty reported to the agency director through one other official, and ten reported through two or more agency officials. One group, because of a reorganization, changed from reporting through one to two levels. Summarizing, the typical group tended to be small, located in or composing a "planning and research" office, and close to the director of the agency.

Relations with Field Sites

Out of forty-six groups, cordial relations were maintained with twenty-eight from initial contact through 1971. This often means that cordial relations were maintained through a change in administration, changes in group leaders, changes in contact persons, and changes in organization and mission. In one group there was slowly over four years a complete change in personnel, location, and mission. I do not know of any other research study in government that enjoys such positive relations with so many agencies over a comparable period of time.

Five sites were abandoned because of the lack of management science activities. In one of these, the contact person had already left when we visited him. In another we have continued to maintain cordial relations to this day, although the group is not considered an active field site. In a third of these five we reinitiated relations several years later and found that our initial judgment had been correct.

Seven groups were abolished or had their management scientists leave. In three of them no continuing management science activity related to the discontinued one was identified. In four of these cases, contact either already existed elsewhere in the agency or it was initiated with a staff which assumed some of the duties of the discontinued one. In three cases limitations of time and money prevented maintenance of contact. Since most of the interviews, especially after 1968, had to be conducted by the author, who was employed full time, field visits became difficult to arrange.

In only three cases was lack of cooperation a factor in discontinuing field relations. Sufficient data was collected from one on several visits to allow the inclusion of this group in all analyses. In two other cases contact was made late in the field work when resources were not available for proper site development.

**Characteristics of Field Interviews and Other Field
Contacts**

In the course of research for this study, 253 field interviews were
conducted, an additional twenty interview schedules were completed, and the completion of part or all of a complicated questionnaire was obtained from twenty-eight field sites. More detail about
the interviews is given in Appendix A.

Semistructured Interviews

Two hundred and thirty-two semistructured interviews were completed in the forty-six potential management science activities. An
additional sixteen interviews were conducted in five additional organizations which were contacted for general information about
government management science, and many of these interviews
contained information about specific field sites. Five interviews
were conducted in the Civil Service Commission, regarding its training programs in PPBS, for a total of 253 interviews.

I conducted 125 of the 232 semistructured interviews and sixty-
seven were conducted by Dr. David Tansik. Transcripts were prepared for all 253 interviews, and sometimes more than one researcher participated in an interview. In 12 percent of the interviews
a second transcript helped the interviewers check their notetaking
for thoroughness and accuracy.

The 232 semistructured interviews at field sites were conducted
between May 1967 and April 1972, 40 percent of them in 1967. This
does not mean that the data is that heavily biased toward that year.
Rather, in succeeding years, structured interviews and questionnaires were used extensively, while in 1967 and 1968 the only structured instrument used was a two-page personal history form.

The semistructured interviews were guided by a list of seventeen
information areas, which are listed in Table 4-3.

The 253 semistructured interviews over a five-year period gave
me a perspective on the nature and development of management
science activities in federal agencies and provided the basis for
structured instruments which were developed later. They also gave
us confidence that the answers to items on these instruments would
be honest and complete, as well as providing a means for checking
consistency of response in all varieties of field contact.

Table 4-3
Seventeen Information Categories for the Conduct of Semistructured
Interviews

1. Personnel and their backgrounds
2. Staff location and reorganization
3. Origin and history of the staff
4. Mission of the staff
5. Current projects underway; past projects
6. Project selection procedures and criteria
7. Top management support
8. Client relations
9. Relations with other staff groups
10. Characteristics of supporters and resisters of the staff and its activity
11. Reputation of the staff in the agency
12. Other management science activity in the agency elsewhere known to respondent
13. Recruitment, departures, training, and professional activities
14. Resources: data, money, computers, slots, and grades
15. Communications
16. Internal relations and organization
17. Miscellaneous

Structured Interviews and Questionnaires

Four types of structured instruments were used in the field. The most important was a large questionnaire distributed in 1971. Second, there was a long instrument that was used in interviewing sixteen agency directors, deputy directors, and other senior officers. A complicated instrument for the measurement of project complexity was administered on a pilot basis, but field time could not be obtained for further use of it. Finally, during 1967 and 1968 the leaders of all activities contacted were asked to distribute to their subordinates a two-page personal experience history form which included questions about present task assignments. One hundred twenty-three forms were returned and were available in later stages of this study.[3] Similar forms were used as part of the "1971 questionnaire."

The "1971 questionnaire" was designed to measure variables relevant to the description of the development of management science activities and yielded voluminous data, with high return rate.

The questionnaire is in three parts. First, there is a fixed-length general section in which information is sought on such matters as the name and location of the staff, the names of all staff professionals, computer availability, top management support for the staff, client relations and implementation problems, staff budget and personnel expansion plans, and staff orientation toward clients. The second part consists of a two-page personal history form, seeking information from each staff member about his or her education, work experience, publications, and present task assignments. The last part consists of two-page project description forms which are simplified versions of the *Project Complexity Measurement Schedule*. On these forms are questions about the title of the project, client, beginning and ending dates for the project, source of project initiation, techniques used, professional man-months devoted to the project, its yield of implementable results and the fate of those results, and the complexity of the project as the respondent perceived it and as he or she felt the client perceived it.

The questions were all designed to elicit information about one or another of five specific variables which are used to describe the history of management science activities in Chapters 2 and 3. A set of the 1971 questionnaire forms is found in Appendix B.

In January and February 1971 these forms were distributed to twenty-eight field sites and in June forms were distributed to four more. The overall return rate was 75 percent of the sets fully completed and an additional 12.5 percent partially completed, not including the one respondent who sent a letter. Only three of the thirty-two activities solicited declined to make any response.

The *Top Management Interview Schedule* was used in 1969 to study the attitudes and behavior of agency top managers toward management science in general. The instrument has thirteen sections and runs twenty-five pages. It usually took at least one and a half hours to administer. The thirteen sections cover a wide range of attitudes and experiences. Specific questions cover the areas or types of problems to which management science and the specific management science activity can and/or does contribute; about the manager's communication with the management science staff through liaison persons, written reports, or oral reports on a periodic or irregular basis, or specific, nonroutine interventions such as conflict mediation or resolution; about the manager's evaluation of the activity on a number of direct and indirect variables; and about occasions in which the activity's outputs or behaviors have had specific impact on the manager's own behavior, decision-making, or attitudes. For this last category of information, critical event probes are used to bring specific recent events to the surface. The questioning strategy then leads the respondent toward assessing the representativeness of these events. Critical event probes were used because I wanted to learn about top managers' behavior as well as their attitudes. I also wanted to give them an opportunity to ground evaluative and attitudinal responses in specific experiences.

Interviews with agency top managers were obtained with little difficulty. Sixteen agency directors were approached by letter and then telephone in July 1969; interviews were arranged and conducted with eight of the sixteen in late July or early August of that year. In two agencies the director arranged for me to interview the deputy director, and in one of these agencies both the incumbent and the recently retired deputy were interviewed. In five agencies interviews were arranged with officials at the level of assistant director. In only one agency was it impossible to obtain an interview.

The *Project Complexity Measurement Schedule* represents an attempt to measure a large number of dimensions of management science projects in the hope of identifying those few which best predicted the response of clients to projects. Although it was only pilot tested in the field, the schedule influenced me in developing the project description forms for the 1971 questionnaire.[4]

The schedule is adaptable to projects of varying complexity, with respect to the number of techniques and submodels or the number of different roles and tasks in the project team. Depending on these factors, the nineteen-page instrument may have overall as many as 100 items.

The schedule was pilot tested in four field sites in August and September 1969. It worked as an interview schedule but could not be left as a questionnaire. In responding to it as a questionnaire, respondents would search their files for precise figures on staff time, computer usage, etc., rather than estimate as they would during an interview; this proved burdensome.

Other Features of Field Contact

Three other aspects of field relations should be mentioned. These are frequency of field contact, documents obtained from field sites, and feedback sessions and workshop conferences with field respondents. They complete the presentation about field methods.

Frequency of contact. More than one interview might be conducted during a site visit, and during a site visit a semistrucutred interview might be conducted before a structured instrument was administered or left with the interviewee. Overall, many sites had ten or more field contacts. Those for which there were fewer generally fall into one of three categories: no management science activity was found; the activity was discontinued within a year or so of first contact; or the activity was first contacted late in the study. Site visits were attempted annually, but resources did not always permit that. Appendix A offers further detail on frequency of contact.

Documents. A variety of documents were obtained from the field sites; in many, project reports were obtained. When this was possible, it provided an opportunity for interviewers to compare these documents with what they had recorded in interview transcripts. In two cases staff histories prepared for professional conferences were obtained. On a number of occasions internal memoranda or agency newsletters were given to us, and at one field site we were given an extensive series of newsletters and memos from the staff's early years. A total of about fifty documents were obtained, many of which were useful supplements to field interviews and questionnaires because they allowed the interviewers to identify misperceptions in interviews and become sensitive to general biases of the respondents.

Feedback sessions and workshop conferences. The research program of which this study was a part was joint sponsor of two conferences for government management scientists. The first was held in December 1968. About half of the time was devoted to workshop discussions of organizational and behavioral problems of conducting management science in government, while the other half was devoted to guest speakers and presentations of preliminary research results by members of the research program.

In September 1969 a one-day conference was held in Washington, where several papers were presented by prominent figures in the management science community and discussed by members of the research program and by government management scientists. In addition to these workshop conferences, members of the research program regularly fed back research results to the management science community through papers delivered at professional society meetings. Criticism and suggestions were solicited and received.

The diversity of field methods continually provided opportunities to verify the accuracy of interviewers' perceptions and new ideas. This diversity also posed the problem of how to process the resulting data systematically.

The Coding Process

The phase model was developed to its current degree of explicitness in order to attempt to turn it from a personal metaphor into a replicable description. If the phase model approximates an underlying order in the histories of management science activities, a second observer, using the same data available to me, should be able to arrive independently at the same phase description of those histories. These descriptions would include the same phases in the same sequence and of about the same duration that I found. The coding process is one way such a comparison can be made.

The coding process involved two stages, the first of which was the coding of the five variables for each management science activity. The second was to use the first-stage coding and Table 3-2 to assign the activities to phases. I and a colleague did the coding in 1971 at Northwestern University. The details of this coding are given in the dissertation on which this book is based. Here the coding process will be summarized, and conclusions about the model and the coding process will be drawn.

In the coding process my colleague, here called "the coder," was first instructed in the definitions of the variables and phases, and in the use of a coding form. Each coding involved first, the reading of all the available interview transcripts and other documents; then trying to arrive at an overall view of the activity's state at a point in time; and only then assigning values to the five variables at that point in time. The variables were coded at quarter-year intervals, although there was a tendency to focus particularly closely on periods when the values seemed to be changing. Thirty management science activities were coded on the five-variable scheme. The first was done collaboratively and the other twenty-nine independently. As much as possible, disagreements were resolved by discussion after each activity was coded.

Intercoder Agreement

Five and one-fourth years was the average period for which each of the twenty-nine activities was coded. With each activity being coded on five variables for each quarter, there were 3,040 coding items. Of this number there were 257 disagreements (8.45 percent) of which seventy-nine (2.60 percent) were left unresolved after discussion. Since the purpose of the coding was to code activities into phases, this raw coding agreement is less important than is a discussion of the number of activities for which there are disputed phases.

When Table 3-2 is used with the codings of the five variables to make assignments of phases, the unresolved disagreements in the coding of the five variables cause no differences in phase assignments for twenty-three of the twenty-nine independently coded management science activities. In four of the activities there are a total of five disagreements about the assignment of phases, all of which involve a period of less than one year. In only two of the twenty-nine activities does disagreement on the coding of the five variables lead to disagreements about phase assignments of four or more quarters' length, and there is only one such disagreement in each of these two activities. If each of the twenty-nine activities is considered to begin in the general phase of *penentration and initial organization* and move from there through a succession of subphases, there are a total for all twenty-nine of ninety-five phase changes. The five shorter disagreements affect *when* a phase change occurs; the two longer disagreements affect *what* phase a particular change is to.

Interpreting Intercoder Agreement

It is difficult to arrive at a measure of coding reliability comparable to the normal percentage agreement measure. The situation here is complicated by the importance of agreement on when phase changes occur, as well as to what phase the change is made, by the two-stage nature of the coding process in which disagreement on the five-variable scheme need not lead to differences in phases, and by the stability of most of the variables most of the time, which makes raw-coding agreement misleading. Out of ninety-five phase changes, however, there is dispute about the timing *or* the nature of only seven, less than 10 percent. Therefore, if the coding and verification performed here is as replicable as I think it is, the phase model allows the development of management science activities to be described commonly by different people. The phases themselves may reflect an underlying order in the development of management science activities.

The coding process was applied to the diverse interview and questionnaire data from those groups for which data was plentiful over a period of several years. The result is a history of each of these groups as a pattern of phases. In the next chapter these histories will be presented and examined.

5 Patterns in the Development, Adoption, and Diffusion of Management Science in Government

The descriptive phase model of Chapter 3 can be used to present the histories of individual management science activities. These histories, it should be remembered, can be viewed from the perspective of the management scientists or from that of the agency—as the development of a management science activity or as the adoption of management science as a sociotechnical innovation. A number of activity histories have been coded into the model's phases. This data is used to explore and compare experiences that management science activities were having at points several years apart. This leads to conclusions with implications for research on the diffusion of complex innovations.

Patterns of Development of Government Management Science Activities

The histories of thirty-three federal, civilian agency management science activities have been coded into the model's phases.[1] Several groups of patterns can be noted, although it is rare to find two activities with identical patterns. Figure 5-1 shows four types of patterns based on the evolutionary and revolutionary distinction suggested in Chapter 2 and on the notion of tentative legitimacy proposed later in that chapter.

The development-adoption patterns of thirty-three activities will be examined through these four categories after each type has been discussed briefly. In the second part of this chapter, the thirty-three coded histories will be used to explore changes over time in the sample as a whole.

The thirty-three activities show a variety of patterns, some of which are complicated. Unlike the adoption process for simple technical innovations, in these patterns, phases may be repeated, traversed in different orders, or skipped.

Twenty-two of the thirty-three activities are easily classified

	activity begins with tentative legitimacy	activity begins with no legitimacy
revolutionary	R_L	R
evolutionary	E_L	E

Figure 5-1. Four Types of Patterns Through the Phase Model of the Development of Management Science Activities

according to either a revolutionary or evolutionary pattern, as the terms are defined here. There are eight activities which follow the phases of first one and then the other of these two patterns, and there are three activities whose development histories are even more complex. Within these two major patterns a distinction will be made between the activities that are coded to begin in a consolidating legitimacy phase and those that are not. Only among the activities not clearly revolutionary or evolutionary is a pattern similar to that proposed by Radnor and Rubenstein (see Figure 2-1), found more than occasionally.

In Figures 5-2 through 5-11, the diagram of phases presented in Figure 3-2 has been simplified to facilitate drawing between phases the arrows that will trace the patterns. The general phases first presented in Table 3-2 and discussed in Chapter 3 are given in the left column of Figure 5-2. The boxes in the figure, and others like it, contain the names of the subphases within those general phases. The data presented in Figures 5-5 through 5-11 are the result of the coding process discussed in Chapter 4. In those figures the numbers in circles identify activities by their file numbers.

Revolutionary and evolutionary patterns are distinguished by the phases they include. For a group to be in the revolutionary pattern it must pass through a missionary phase and/or a rapid consolidation phase. It must not pass through either of the corresponding phases of gradual consolidation or development of organizational role. For a group to be classified as evolutionary, it must pass through either or both of the latter phases, but it cannot pass through any of the former phases. Still, in each pattern, this leaves a number of possibilities open, some of which are illustrated in Figures 5-2 (the revolutionary pattern) and 5-3 (the evolutionary pat-

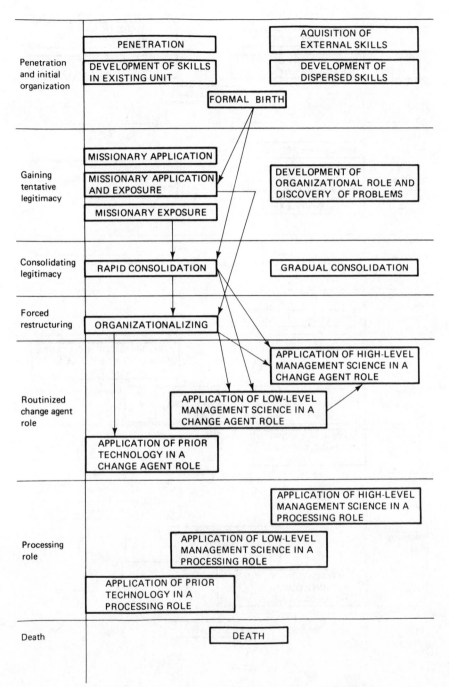

Figure 5-2. Examples of Revolutionary Patterns

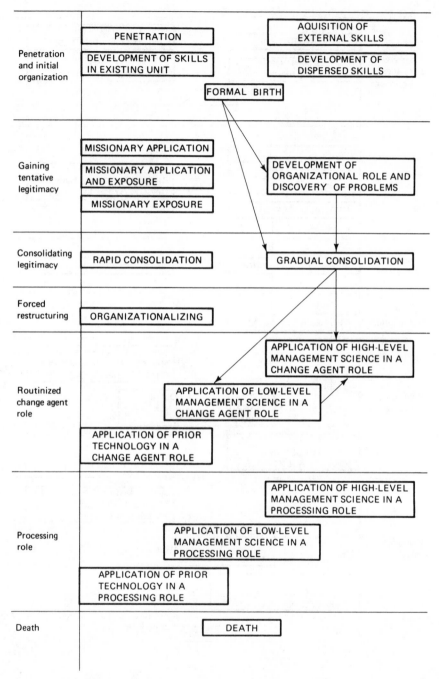

Figure 5-3. Examples of Evolutionary Patterns

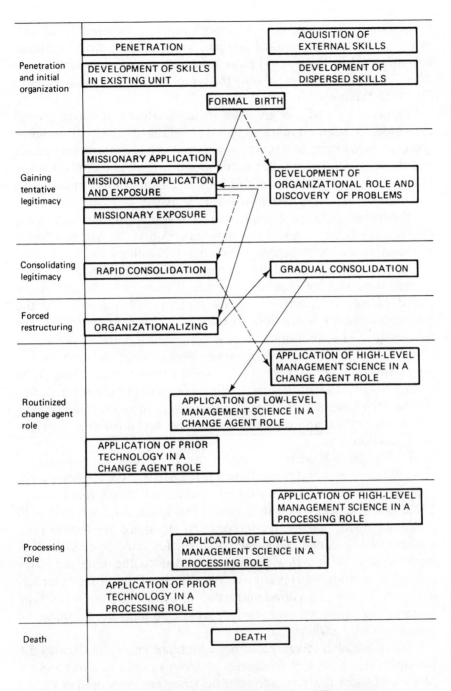

Figure 5-4. Two Examples of Mixed Patterns

tern). When an activity passes through phases characteristic of both major patterns, it is a mixed pattern. Some simple, mixed patterns are indicated in Figure 5-4; more complex, actual ones are shown later. These figures present only the connecting arrows necessary to illustrate the patterns.

Figures 5-5 and 5-6 give the actual patterns of those groups classified as revolutionary. The two figures distinguish between groups which begin their revolutionary pattern in a missionary phase and those which begin (after initial organization) in a consolidation phase. Only two of a total of thirty-three groups show a revolutionary pattern and start with a missionary phase.

When data collection stopped in 1972 neither of these activities, which have been assigned file numbers 35 and 36, had reached a phase of applying management science technology in a *routinized change agent* role. Seven groups begin their revolutionary patterns in the *consolidating legitimacy* phase (Figure 5-6). In 1971 their coded phases included one death and several examples of the *routinized change agent* role with *high-level management science technology*. The total number of revolutionary patterns is nine.

In Figure 5-7 are shown the seven evolutionary patterns, beginning with the *gaining tentative legitimacy* phase. According to the coding results, two of these activities were still in the *consolidating legitimacy* phase in 1971. Several others were in a *routinized change agent role* phase, and the others no longer had a management science mission.

In Figure 5-8 activities coded as beginning in a phase of *consolidating legitimacy* are shown. Five of these six activities were applying management science in a *routinized change agent* role in 1971, and the sixth was in a *routinized change agent* role with premanagement science technology. In all, there are thirteen activities whose coded development histories can be classified as evolutionary. When this number is added to the nine activities following revolutionary patterns, two-thirds of the thirty-three activities have been classified into either of these two patterns. Of the twenty-two, thirteen are coded as beginning in a phase of *consolidating legitimacy*.

There are also mixed patterns, which are shown in Figures 5-9 through 5-11. Seven of these eleven groups begin in a *missionary* phase and show fairly simple patterns (they are presented in Figure 5-9). Five of the seven pass through the *forced restructuring* phase,

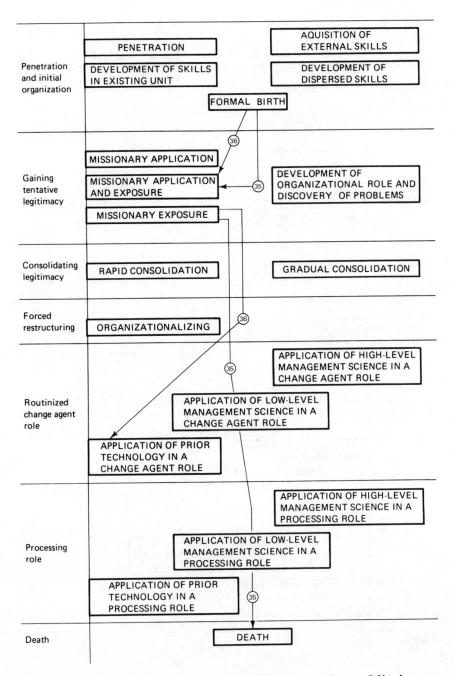

Figure 5-5. Revolutionary Patterns Beginning in a Missionary Phase

64

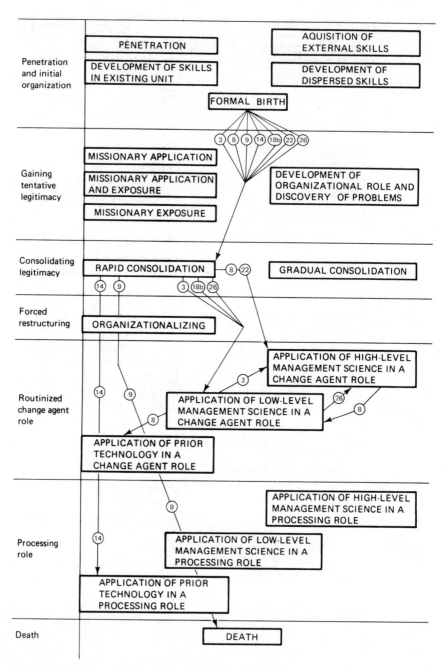

Figure 5-6. Revolutionary Patterns Beginning in a Consolidating Phase

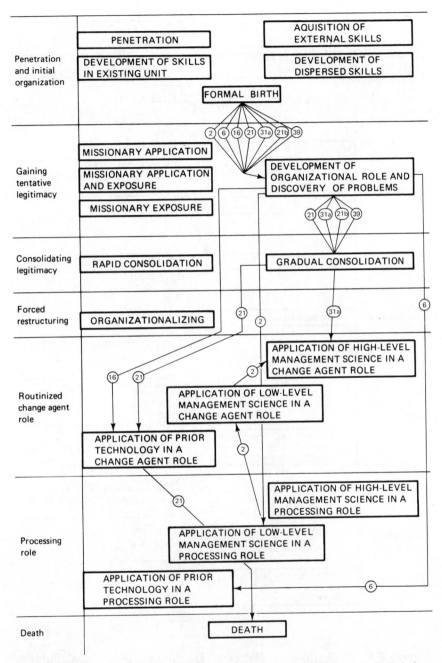

Figure 5-7. Evolutionary Patterns Beginning in a Phase of Gaining Tentative Legitimacy

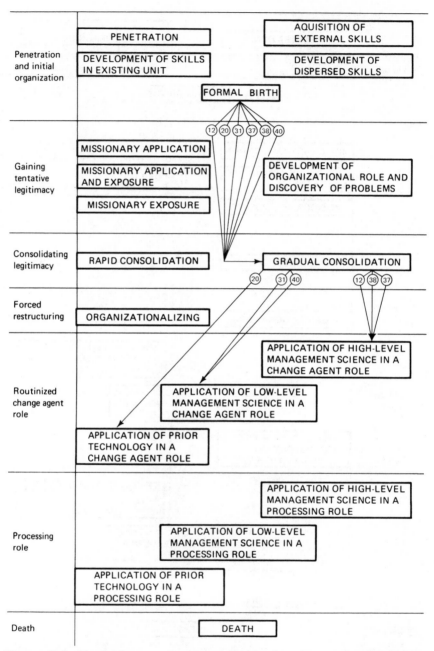

Figure 5-8. Evolutionary Patterns Beginning in a Consolidating Phase

one of them twice. Two others, numbers 13 and 34, go directly from one of the characteristic revolutionary phases to characteristic evolutionary phases. Of the seven, three were coded in 1971 in a *routinized change agent role* phase, three in the *gradual consolidation* phase, and one in the evolutionary phase, *development of organizational role*. In Figure 5-10 there is only one group, a mixed pattern beginning in the *rapid consolidation* phase but passing through both *gradual and rapid consolidation*. Finally, in Figure 5-11 there are three more complex mixed patterns. Group numbers 1 and 19 are especially complex, passing through six or seven phases each. Of the eleven groups coded as having mixed patterns, nine begin with a *missionary* phase, one begins with a *rapid consolidation* phase, and one begins in the evolutionary pattern.

Among the thirty-three government management science activities, those coded as having mixed development patterns follow most closely the phases of Radnor's and Rubenstein's model (see Figure 2-1). Activities numbered 10, 15, 17, 23, and 28b can all be traced in Figure 5-9 through an initial surge (*missionary* phases), a decline (*organizationalizing*), and then a gradual recovery (*gradual consolidation* and/or *development of organizational* role) toward what they call "maturity" (application of management science in a *routine change agent* role). In support of that early model, it should be noted that in these five activities, along with numbers 1 and 19, some of the earliest formally chartered government management science was performed. On the basis of interviews, the initiation of each of these activities can be located before 1966. Few of the newer activities were coded into patterns similar to that implied by the Radnor-Rubenstein model, which was proposed in the form presented here in the mid-1960s on the basis of research on industrial management science activities.

Recorded in Chapter 2 is a decision to seek a phase model more complex than the Radnor-Rubenstein model. The presentation here of the coded development histories of thirty-three federal civilian agency management science activities tends to support that decision. The successful, verified coding of these activities into the phases of the model indicates that there are diverse but recognizable patterns of development-adoption in government agencies. While simpler innovations may be adopted through relatively unvarying processes, management science clearly is not. This finding implies

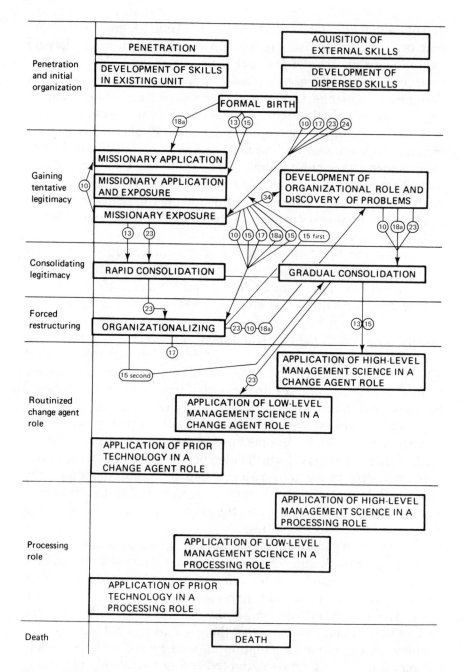

Figure 5-9. Seven Mixed Patterns, Each Beginning in a Missionary Phase

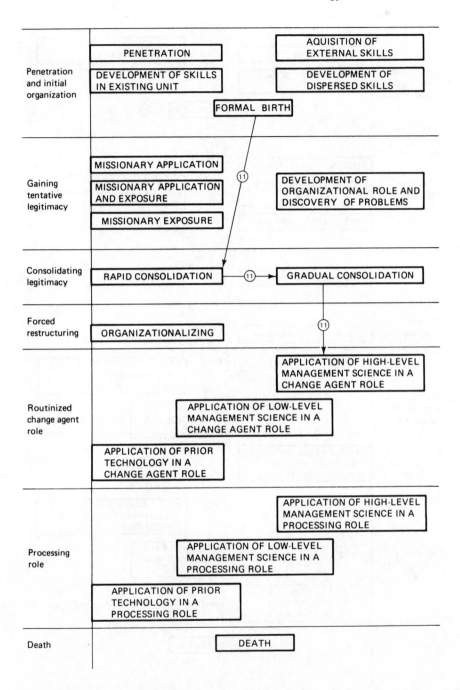

Figure 5-10. A Mixed Pattern Beginning in a Consolidating Phase

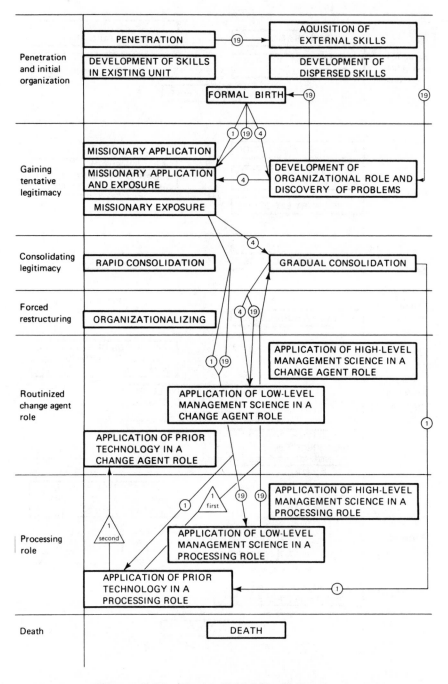

Figure 5-11. Three Odd Mixed Patterns

that further research may be warranted on previously well-studied innovations such as agricultural techniques and drugs.

The four development-adoption patterns are related to research on the adoption of simple innovations. The distinction between *tentative* and *no legitimacy* (Figures 5-1 and 2-3) is related to Rogers' formulation. Implied is that under certain conditions, the early phases in Rogers' scheme are completed before there is active consideration of adoption. I have not found a distinction between evolutionary and revolutionary patterns in other literature. One reason for this is that the choice among these two alternatives is largely determined by the management scientists, that is, by the innovation itself. Simple technical innovations, as opposed to sociotechnical innovations, being impersonal, cannot act on the adopting organization. When the adoption of an innovation involves the introduction of new specialist roles—which is the case with computers, organizational development, affirmative action, futurology, and many other products of modern thought—the findings presented here regarding the development and adoption of management science activities may be an illuminating precedent.

Temporal Perspectives on the Development and Adoption of Management Science Activities in Government

In treating the development and adoption of management science activities as an example of the diffusion of a sociotechnical innovation, we must examine changes in adoption patterns over a period of time. This will also suggest some contingencies associated with the various patterns. Assuming some degree of representativeness in the sample of thirty-three management science activities, four aggregate hypotheses about these patterns are suggested.

First, management science was established in many government agencies before the issuance of the Budget Bureau's *Bulletin* No. 66-3 on October 12, 1965. This bulletin ordered the immediate implementation of the planning-programming-budgeting system in federal departments and many federal agencies. It is sometimes seen as being the initial reason for management science activities in federal civilian agencies. Immediately after its issuance there was an acceleration in the initiation of new civilian agency management science activities. Second, during the 1960s the length of time between the initiation of a management science activity in a federal civilian agency and the attainment by that activity of a *routinized change agent role* phase involving the use of management science technology tended to decrease. Third, in the latter part of the 1960s management science activities increasingly began in a *consolidating legitimacy* phase. Fourth, in the late 1960s new activities more often began in evolutionary rather than revolutionary phases, while in the first half of the decade the opposite held. Evidence suggesting these hypotheses is presented in Figures 5-12 through 5-16. These last two hypotheses have broad research implications.

Figure 5-12 presents the phases into which each of the activities has been coded for the end of years 1960 through 1970. Fourteen of the thirty-three activities (42 percent) existed by the end of 1965. The two added to the sample that year originated well before the planning-programming-budgeting system (PPBS) was announced. It is not clear whether that announcement catalyzed or caused the accelerated growth of management science activity hypothesized here.

Figure 5-12 also shows that the fraction of the thirty-three activities coded as applying management science in a *routinized change agent role* phase increases substantially in the latter half of the decade. This may result partly from the simple increase in the size of the sample, but it should also be from the more rapid development of new activities to those phases. In figure 5-13 evidence is presented which supports the latter hypothesis. For example, the activities beginning in 1966 or 1967 can be compared with those beginning before that time. Ten of the sixteen begun in that two-year period reached a *routinized change agent role* phase in three years or less; only two of the fourteen earlier activities did that.

The bar graphs in Figure 5-14 show beginning phases for activities based on the distinction between beginning with no legitimacy (in a phase of *gaining tentative legitimacy*) and tentative legitimacy (in a phase of *consolidating legitimacy*). In 1966 and 1967 more of the activities began in the latter type of phase, while in other years more began in the former type. The evidence is scanty for recent years. Over the years the trend within federal agencies, for new management science activities to begin in a phase of consolidating legitimacy, may indicate that a favorable orientation toward management science has spread within these organizations. This, in turn, suggests that at an aggregate level, management science activities in organizations might profitably be studied as a case of diffusion of innovation even if the adoption process is complex.

A general hypothesis about the diffusion of complex sociotechnocal innovations is suggested when the thirty-three management science activities are examined to see whether there is any change in the relative frequency of revolutionary and evolutionary phases over time. Examination of activities coded in either the revolutionary or the evolutionary alternatives of the phases, *gaining tentative legitimacy* and *consolidating legitimacy*, suggests a trend during the 1960s from revolutionary to evolutionary activity for government management science (Figure 5-15). In the sample those activities alive in the early years of civilian agency management science are more often coded as being in revolutionary phases; in the latter part of the decade evolutionary phases are more common. As a whole, then, the sample is characterized by revolutionary activity in the early years and evolutionary activity later on. Extending this finding to all management science activities in a family of organizations suggests a general hypothesis about the diffusion of managerial technologies and other complex sociotechnical innovations: adoption in the early years of diffusion is characterized more often by revolutionary activity and in later years more often by evolutionary activity. I suspect that there is a change in the nature of adoption processes as diffusion progresses.

Some Notes Toward a Theory of the Adoption and Diffusion of Sociotechnical Innovations

The concept of the adoption process as being variable is critical to the idea of diffusion. Adoption processes can be seen as being variable only if they are described by a fairly complex process model. The phase model used in this book was developed from an intensive study of a relatively large number of cases. Its sixteen phases were articulated to describe the richness of field experience, which had forced me away from simpler models.

Referring again to Figure 5-1, four types of adoption processes for complex, sociotechnical innovations can be identified. These are supplemented by idiosyncratic cases which fit no recognizable pattern. First, adoption processes can be evolutionary or revolution-

Phase \\ Year	1960	1961	1962	1963	1964	1965	1966	1967	1968	1969	1970
Missionary Exposure			17	17	17,23	17	35	34,35	35,36	35,36	
Missionary Application and Exposure			15,	1,15	1,15	15,19					
Missionary Application						10	28a	4			
Gradual Development	2,31a	2,31a	31a	31,31a, 19	21,31a, 19	21	4,10	10,16,23	10,16,28a, 21b,23,34	28a,21b, 34,39	34,39
Rapid Consolidation	13,14	14	14,22	14,22	14,22	14,23, 26	8,9,11, 23	3,9,11, 18b	18b	18b	
Gradual Consolidation		13	13	13	13	13,31a	1,12,15, 19,21,40 31a,38,	15,17,19, 20,31a,21, 37,40	4,15,17, 19,20,21, 37,40	10,17,23, 31,37	10,17,28a, 21b, 23
Organizationalizing							17	28a			
High-Level Management Science in Change Agent Role						22	13,22	8,12,13, 22,26,38	2,11,12, 13,31a,22, 26,38	2,11,12, 13,15,31a, 22,26,38	2,3,11,12, 15,31a,22, 26,37,38
Low-Level Management Science in Change Agent Role					2	2	2,26	2	3,8	3,4,8, 19,40	4,18b,19, 31,40

Prior Technology in Change Agent Role								21	1,16,20,21	1,8,10,20,36
High-Level Management Science in Processing Role										
Low-Level Management Science in Processing Role		2	2							
Prior Technology in a Processing Role	6	6	6	6	1,6	6,14	1,6,14	1,6,14	6,14	6,14
Death								9	9	9,21,35
Don't Know							31			
Total Groups Active at End of Year	5	8	11	12	14	23	30	32	33	33

*End of the year phases for the groups: numbers are surrogates for the names of the groups; chart allows reader to follow the progress of individual group over the years.

Figure 5-12. End-of-Year Phases for Each of Thirty-three Federal Civilian Agency Management Science Activities, 1960-70.*

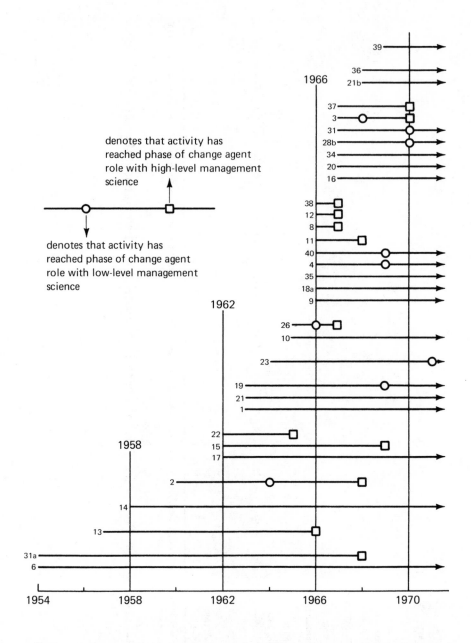

Figure 5-13. Number of Years from Initiation to Routine Application of Management Science in a Change Agent Role

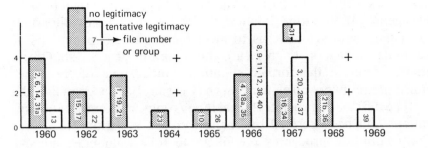

Figure 5-14. Management Science Activities Beginning in Each Year, Divided into Those Which Begin with No Legitimacy and Those Which Begin with Tentative Legitimacy

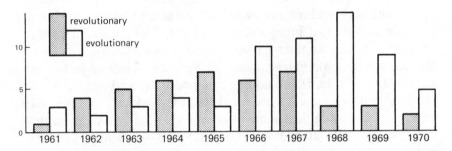

Figure 5-15. Number of Management Science Activities in Revolutionary or Evolutionary Phases, by Year

ary. In the former, the process is characterized by gradual development of the sociotechnical innovation, responsiveness to organizational parameters, and little conflict between innovation and the adopting agency. In the latter case, the innovators act aggressively on the adopting agency, stretch the adaptive capacity of their host, and are often surrounded by conflict and controversy. Second, adoption processes can begin with little legitimacy being granted by the managers in the adopting agency or with some tentative legitimacy granted by the managers. In the former situation, both the technology and the carriers of the technology may be feared, misunderstood, or resisted—the innovators must prove their right to be in the agency. In the latter situation, the challenge for innovators such as management scientists is to meet the positive expectations of adopting managers. In this case the adoption process should be shorter than in the former situation, since some of the time-consuming conversion of managers has already been accomplished.

The diffusion of sociotechnical innovations in a family of organizations can be described by changes in the adoption processes. Early adoption processes are likely to follow complicated and idiosyncratic patterns such as those in Figures 5-9 through 5-11. Later, revolutionary patterns will emerge as characteristic. After several years evolutionary patterns will become more common. A parallel development is that the adoption process itself becomes shorter as time passes. One reason for this may be that the late-adopting agencies will not allow introduction of the social component of the sociotechnical innovation until some tentative legitimacy has developed. But independently of this, the adoption process becomes shorter as time passes, perhaps because the innovators themselves become more socially skilled and sensitive to the subtleties of their role. It should be remembered from Figure 5-12 that these adoption processes are measured in years and that the diffusion of a sociotechnical innovation such as management science, begun in the 1950s in federal civilian agencies, was still playing itself out almost twenty years later.

6

Management Science and the Study of Organizational Change in Public Administration

The approach to research on management science used in this study is empirical rather than normative, longitudinal rather than cross-sectional, comparative rather than a case study. This approach offers advantages over the other research approaches that have been used, such as speculative consideration, case studies, or cross-sectional comparisons. While speculative evaluations may produce interesting questions, the importance of empirical investigation need hardly be emphasized. The speculations of the wise and experienced may eventually be confirmed, while an empirical orientation helps to contain the wild, extravagant, foolish, or facetious. Other common methods of research deprive the researcher and reader of perspective and therefore of context. Reasonable judgments about the likely acceptance or impact of management science can be made either by the gifted or by those with observational experience extended both in space and time.

Speculative Reaction to Management Science

In recent years social scientists have reacted sharply to the introduction of modern management science techniques and systems into civilian government. Operations research, systems analysis, microeconomic analysis and the planning-programming-budgeting system have been greeted with a mixture of derision and fear. Bluntly put, some political scientists have stated that these techniques and systems cannot solve government problems. Wildavsky, for example, states that PPBS cannot be done because no one knows how to do it.[1] Victor Thompson considers these techniques and systems an attempt to replace politics with science. He argues that "science cannot solve social problems," the solutions to which are described instead by words like "compromise, consensus, majority, negotiations, bargaining, coercion, etc." According to Thompson, "If the 'solution' cannot be described in such terms, then it is not the

79

solution of a social problem." He feels that "econologicians" vastly underestimate the complexity of social phenomena, an opinion shared by Frederick C. Mosher.

Political scientists have offered a variety of criticisms of management science when, or if, it is used in civilian government policy-formation. Wildavsky argues that benefit-cost analyses can be "fudged" through the invention of intangible benefits, manipulation of the discount rate, or opportunistic aggregation. Mosher feels that PPBS is too market-oriented. Richard Fenno suggests that budget reform proposals, many of which reflect management science thinking, are rejected by legislators who feel the proposals are unlikely "to help them perform their function any better." Thompson feels that management scientists will ignore critical variables in their search for a determinate solution and solve the easy rather than the significant problems. Wildavsky comments on the difficulty of encompassing diverse objectives in a single-criterion function and of making interpersonal comparisons of utility. He argues that we have political rather than economic mechanisms for handling the latter in government. Bertram Gross fears that management science analysis will paralyze government.

The elaborate and articulate theories of economist Charles E. Lindblom provide these individual comments with an encompassing theoretical framework. His theories of incremental decision-making were formulated partly as a response to the idea of comprehensive national planning: specifics of his theories contradict ideas usually seen as basic to management science. For example, Lindblom argues for the consideration of only those few alternatives that are marginally different from present policy. He also argues that in politics, participants should keep their goals concealed in order to facilitate agreement, whereas in management science, goal clarification and explicit formulation is important.[2] Lindblom also argues that incremental decision-making involves many people, its openness to diverse sources of information being a major value. Management science, critics assume, will restrict participation and be antidemocratic. Wildavsky, for example, thinks "normative budget theories" are totalitarian, and Bertram Gross sees systems analysis promoting social discontinuity and disorder.

There is an ambiguity in these comments. Wildavsky, Thompson, Fenno, and Mosher imply that management science cannot contribute effectively to the solution of governmental problems. But

Lindblom, Wildavsky, and others fear that management science may contribute to governmental paralysis, social disorder, or tyranny. The political scientists quoted seem to have some difficulty in deciding whether management science can be dismissed as ineffective or should be watched as dangerous.

These comments can be evaluated through the adoption-diffusion perspective of this study. One reason for the ambiguity is that at the time these comments were written, few, if any, of these critics had spent enough time with a real flesh-and-blood management scientist in a government agency to get beneath the optimism characteristic of this emerging profession. In addition, these were early reactions to management science activities which were new, lacking in legitimacy, experiencing turbulent organizational histories, and needing perhaps to oversell just to be heard. The reactions were to rhetoric and not to the agency experiences of management scientists.

With a longitudinal, comparative perspective we can see that ambitious claims, though common when management science was relatively new in federal civilian agencies, were not associated with all management science activities. Those in evolutionary patterns of development-adoption were unlikely to be producing the kinds of claims that would alarm social scientists. In perspective we can see that some management science activities were terminated and others became influential with agency management. Some took many years to become influential and accepted, while others took only a few years.

Further research is needed to clarify the contingencies on which the success of management science activities is dependent. Within the boundaries set by those problems to which management science has little to contribute and those management science contributions that would be found consensually offensive to republican values lies a wide range of problems and contributions contingent upon matters of organizational behavior, political skill, and technical competence.

Case and Cross-Sectional Studies

Case studies, like speculative criticism, offer questions, not answers.[3] The most detailed case study of a management science experience in a federal agency is by Mosher and Harr.[4] They present efforts of some "missionary" State Department administrators on behalf of several innovations partaking of either the principles or techniques of management science. While Mosher and Harr suggest many reasons for these innovations being rejected during the period of their study, their case-study approach prevents them from seeing the State Department experience in context with other management science experiences.

In reviewing the Mosher and Harr book, I have argued that the development-adoption experience they portray is common among early management science efforts in a family of organizations. The State Department experience began shortly after 1960, which was early among federal civilian agencies. The temporal perspective that I have gained in the present study suggests that Mosher's and Harr's reasons for the "failure" of management science efforts in the State Department cannot be accepted. Most of the reasons were also present several years later in other agencies in which management science activities achieved organizational influence and acceptance. The Mosher-Harr case should be a warning that in such studies, one is likely to propose explanations under the assumption that a steady state, rather than a transient phenomenon, has occurred. In the study of organizational change, a longitudinal, comparative perspective allows the researcher to isolate the initial, confused organizational responses to disturbance from the more regular adaptations in the longer term.

Another problem with case studies is that they offer repetition rather than cumulation. In the early writings of management scientists, their acceptance in organizations is seen as dependent on production within the context of long-term projects of frequent and immediately useful recommendations.[5] One finds this recommendation a common product of case studies a decade and more later.[6] The repetition may underline the wisdom of the prescription. But longitudinal, comparative research shows that this mixture of long- and short-term work, or "mixed portfolio," is a common stage in the development and adoption process. Radnor et al. find that project portfolio composition shifts as management science activities develop.[7] In a study of 108 industrial management science activities, Michael Radnor and Rodney Neal find a shift over time toward mixed portfolios.[8] A.S. Bean et al. find a mixed portfolio associated with what they call a "missionary" phase, but less so with later phases.[9]

The research of Radnor, Bean, and their colleagues on industrial operations research suggests that the mixed portfolio is the product of and is relevant to an intermediate phase in the development and adoption of management science activities. A weakness of case studies, then, is that recommendations drawn from them in ignorance of broader perspectives may be inappropriate in many of the situations to which they will be applied.

Comparative cross-sectional research can also be informed by the longitudinal perspective of this study. For example, A.S. Bean finds that management scientists misunderstand the support they receive from the top managers of their organizations, support they consider critical.[10] My own research shows that top managers draw from a wide repertory of responses to management science activities.[11] Each of these studies of top management and management science is comparative but cross-sectional. The diffusion-adoption phase model offered here allows the investigation of top management and management science over time. At what stage of development is top management support most important? Most likely to be miscalculated? Is there an association between the phase of development and the way top managers provide support? And the kind of support needed? Top management's relations with management science are a subject for organizational design decisions, as well as for academic research. Propositions derived from longitudinal, comparative field research are likely to be accompanied by the temporal and situational qualifications important to managers attempting to make organizational design decisions.

Implementation of research results is another widely studied aspect of management science, yet rarely has implementation been seen as a function either of the stage of development-adoption of a specific activity or of the extent of diffusion of management science in a particular family of organizations. In cross-sectional research on over 100 industrial management science activities, Bean and his colleagues found that there is substantial change in the factors associated with implementation according to the phase that a group is in.[12] In some phases the firm's environment offers the strongest associations, while in others it is the characteristics of the management science activity itself. They use a phase model related to the one I have proposed in this book. Their phase model has made it possible for them to examine temporal contingencies with cross-sectional data. Continued data collection with their sample may permit verification of their findings with temporal correlations. There may be factors influencing the implementation of research recommendations which operate independently of temporal considerations. David A. Tansik's careful work on the measurability of organizational goals is one example.[13] But any relatively thorough understanding of implementation and of most other important aspects of management science and related organizational change experiences requires temporal specification which is possible only through research that is both comparative and longitudinal.

The concern with implementation may change in nature if not in intensity as management science diffuses throughout a family of organizations and gains general acceptance. Not so long ago, prominent management scientists were wondering whether their work was ever implemented. In recent years prizes have been offered at the joint national meetings of the Institute of Management Sciences and the Operations Research Society of America for the best-implemented management science study. The careful work of Bean et al. and of Neal and Radnor on specific, limited problems in implementation reflects the wide diffusion and acceptance of management science in American industry.[14] Case studies such as those of Ira Lowry, James Storey, and R.E. Park indicate not the limited potential of management science in government but its comparative newness.[15] Those interested in the use of management science in government can gain insight into the changes associated with growing diffusion into government by examining the changes associated with past diffusion into industry.

Research on Management Science and Research in Public Administration

The subject of this study, *the development and adoption of management science activities in government agencies*, shares important features with other subjects of interest to students of governmental activity. It is a process that is evolving over a long period of time. It is composed of many specific experiences, each having an important temporal dimension. And all of this occurs in a complex institutional environment which no single perspective can adequately capture.

Management science activities have been conceptualized on the basis of both adoption and development experiences. A dual perspective on time has also been used. First, management science activities are seen individually as historical experiences. Second, these experiences are then aggregated into a diffusion process encompassing all of them. In the study of public administration one faces the choice of ignoring this complexity or of devising empirical approaches to cope with it. This had been recognized by early researchers in public administration who emphasized two forms of empirical research, the case study and the "capture and record" method. Capture and record was the underlying methodology of the studies of Macmahon, Millet, and Ogden, *The Administration of Federal Work Relief*; Gaus and Wolcott, *Public Administration in the United States Department of Agriculture*; and the Stone, Price, and Stone studies of city managers.[16]

The Social Science Research Council Committee on Public Administration also set in motion activities which resulted in the casewriting activities now continued by Inter-University Case Program, Inc. Harold Stein writes that case studies resulted from a "search for new tools to use in the study of public administration, rather than from any general concern with educational method."[17] He recognizes that the case method, as represented in his book, yields tentative and complex generalizations which are "much less absolute" than those of the physical sciences.[18] He felt that this level of generalization was appropriate to the processes of public administration.

In 1956, however, Frederick C. Mosher reviewed the research tradition in public administration and found it lacking. He argued that public administration had not kept pace with other disciplines: "In those fields associated with behaviors, attitudes, and communications of persons in administrative settings, there appears to be much interest but surprisingly little research contribution on the part of those in the field of public administration."[19] Mosher later tried valiantly to use cases to test hypotheses empirically.[20] However, he urged that there be greater development of and interaction between experimental and field research. In the field of political science only a few scholars have accepted his call for field research of a more sophisticated nature than the case study, although this call was

repeated at greater length and with greater urgency by Robert Presthus in his Southern Regional Training Program lectures almost a
decade later.[21] A review of major scholarly journals in political
science and public administration reveals almost a complete lack of
empirical research on government administration.[22]

In this study I have presented one approach to obtaining systematically what Presthus calls "durational knowledge," knowledge about complex governmental processes. There may be other
approaches, but if we are to understand the complex processes of
public administration, the research approaches will have to involve
data collected in the field, as well as multiple perspectives derived
from spatial and temporal comparisons.

Appendix A
Number and Types of Interviews in Forty-Six Federal Civilian Agency Management Science Activities, 1967-72

File Number of Activity	Dates of First and Most Recent Field Contact	Number of Semistructured Interviews	Top Management Interview	Project Complexity Interview	1971 Questionnaire Returned
1	5/67-9/71	9		Yes	Yes
2	6/67-1/71	5	Yes	Yes	Yes
3	7/67-1/71	3	Yes		Yes
4	7/67-1/71	4			(part)
5	6/67-2/70	5			
6	7/67-7/67	1			
7	7/67-7/67	1			
8	6/67-2/71	3	Yes		
9	6/67-8/68	3			
10	7/67-1/71	8	Yes		Yes
11	7/67-6/71	3			Yes
12	7/67-1/71	7	Yes	Yes	Yes
13	7/67-2/71	17[a]	Yes		Yes
14					
15	6/67-8/73	18	Yes		Yes
16	8/67-1/71	3	Yes		Yes
17	7/67-2/71	11	Yes (two)		Yes
18a	6/67-1/71	6			Yes
19	7/67-6/71	7	Yes	Yes	Yes
20	6/67-2/71	10	Yes		Yes
21	9/67-8/68	4			
21b	8/69-1/71	2			Yes

22	5/67-4/72	3			Yes
23	5/67-1/71	29	Yes	Yes	Yes
24	5/67-1/71	2			(No)
25	6/67-6/67				
26	6/67-4/71	18		Yes	Yes
26c	9/68-9/68	1			(part)
28b	2/69-9/71	7			Yes
31	9/68-1/71	3			Yes
31a	9/67-1/71	6		Yes	Yes
33	8/68-8/68	1			
34	8/68-1/71	3			Yes
35	8/68-8/69	4		Yes	Yes
36	1/69-1/71	3[b]			Yes
37	1/69-8/69	3			Yes
38	1/69-1/71	2			Yes
39	2/70-1/71	2			(part)
40	2/70-1/71	2[b]			(part)
41	2/70-2/70	1			
42	1/71-9/71	2			(part)
43	2/70-1/71	2			(No)
44	6/71-9/71	2			(No)
45	4/71-9/71	2			(No)
46	7/67-7/67	1			
48b	6/71-9/71	2			Yes

[a]Many of these respondents served on and talked about both staffs, and it is not possible to assign interviews exclusively to either.
[b]In addition, I had a staff history which was prepared as a paper for a professional meeting or publication.

Appendix B
Reproduction of the 1971
Questionnaire

General Section
Group Description
January 1971 (revised)

COOPERATIVE INTERNATIONAL PROGRAM OF
STUDIES OF OPERATIONS RESEARCH AND THE
MANAGEMENT SCIENCES
Graduate School of Management
Northwestern University

This section contains mostly questions on general matters. Please complete each item; most can be answered with a word or two at most.

A. Background identification information.

1. Staff name and   _____   Form completed
   organizational   by   _____
   location   _____
                                                   Date   _____
                          _____

   Agency   _____   PLEASE leave this box blank
                                                    Int. by: _____
   Name of staff   with: _____
   leader   _____   t: _____

2. Please list the names of all professionals on this staff (use other side if necessary).

   1. _____   5. _____   9. _____

   2. _____   6. _____   10. _____

   3. _____   7. _____   11. _____

   4. _____   8. _____   12. _____

B. Computer availability.

What machines do you have available?

What is your average turn-around time?

C. Anticipated changes in staff size.

1. Do you anticipate any increases
   In the size of this staff in the
   next year or so?

   Skills and grade levels sought?

2. Do you expect to have this staff
   decreased in size at all in the
   next year or so?

   What skills, and at what grade
   levels do you expect to lose?

91

D. Are there any other staffs in this agency doing analysis, evaluation, or management science work that we might contact?

Name of staff _____   Name of staff _____
                                      leader

_____   _____

E. Below are several statements about the "Top Management Support" that this activity receives. "Top Management" refers to the director and deputy director of the agency. It also refers to any other executives with agency-wide responsibilities except when their responsibilities are *solely* in the field of analysis and evaluation (e.g., an assistant director for program planning and evaluation who himself is the head of this or another management science-type of activity). Please check, for each statement, the appropriate box to its right.

	excellent	good	fair	poor
Top management's interest in and understanding of this activity is				
Top management's help to this activity in getting it the resources it needs is				
Top management's help in arbitrating or resolving intra-agency conflicts in favor of this activity is				
Top management's support in general is				

F. In general, the relations between this staff and other staff groups in this agency are most accurately characterized by which of the following statements? Please check one.

Conflict, hostility, and/or suspicion	
Stress and discomfort	
Mutual tolerance	
Accommodation and occasional cooperation	
Trust, cooperation, and mutual respect	

G. Which of the following statements best describes your orientation toward the "clients" of your work in this agency? Please check one.

We go out and sell ourselves and our skills to the clients	
We wait for the clients to come to us	
We avoid aggressive behavior but take advantage quickly of any interest in our services	

H. Which of the following phrases best describes briefly any problems this staff has in implementing its recommendations? Please check one.

In general this staff has few _____
                     moderate _____
                       severe _____

problems in implementing
its recommendations

I. Staff Budget data. (OPTIONAL)

	current year	past year
What is this staff's approximate budget for the current and for the past fiscal years?	$	$
What *percentage* of this total was reserved for contracts?	%	%

J. Please attach a recent copy of the mission statement for this staff if one is handy. Thank you.

Client Relations Section
Group Description
January 1971 (revised)

COOPERATIVE INTERNATIONAL PROGRAM OF
STUDIES OF OPERATIONS RESEARCH AND THE
MANAGEMENT SCIENCES
Graduate School of Management
Northwestern University

Below are four sets of statements. For each client you list, please choose the statement in each of the four sets of statements that best describes the relations between the client and this activity.

	(Name of Client)	1	2	3	4	5	6	7	8	9
Please list each client (another staff, a line division, a top manager, etc.) in the boxes at the right.										
This client comes to us with project proposals										
will entertain our proposals										
is difficult to get a project going with										
Relations with this client are characterized by conflict, hostility, and/or suspicion										
stress and discomfort										
accommodation and frequent cooperation										
cooperation, trust, and mutual respect										
Regarding the collection of data from this client, we have relatively complete freedom										
we need a general permission										
we need permission for each specific effort										
we can rarely collect data from this operation										
Generally, relations with this client are: Excellent										
Good										
Fair										
Poor										

Project Section
Group Description
January 1971 (revised)

COOPERATIVE INTERNATIONAL PROGRAM OF
STUDIES OF OPERATIONS RESEARCH AND THE
MANAGEMENT SCIENCES
Graduate School of Management
Northwestern University

Please complete one copy of the "Project Section" for each project current or completed in the last 6 to 12 months or for a representative sample of your projects during the same period.

A. Project title and one-sentence description.

B. Project client, if any (please give the name of a person, as well as the name of an organizational unit where possible).

C. In approximately what month and year did this project commence? When was it (will it be) completed?

D. Who initiated this project (check one)?

This staff		The Client	
Another staff group in this agency		Joint, this staff and the client	
A higher manager		Someone outside	
Other		this agency	

E. Major techniques and approaches used.

F. *Approximate* number of man-months on this project, actual or projected. (check appropriate boxes)

Months:	0-4	4-12	12-24	24+
Professional in-house				
contract				
If *implementation* is a major, separate effort, please list separately here				

G. Did the project produce:

	Yes	No
Implementable recommendations regarding changes in systems, procedures, organization, etc.		
Ideas, facts, perspectives, or intelligence relevant to decisions and/or policy		

H. Were those implemented, used or adopted?

	Recommendations	Intelligence
Fully		
Mostly		
Partly		
Little or no use		

Comments:

I. How complex did this staff feel this project was?

(Check here)

Very complex | | | | | | | | | simple

How complex do you feel *the clients* (if any) perceived this project to be?

(Check here)

very complex | | | | | | | | | simple

Personal Data Section JY67
Group Description
January, 1971 (revised)

COOPERATIVE INTERNATIONAL PROGRAM OF
STUDIES OF OPERATIONS RESEARCH AND THE
MANAGEMENT SCIENCES
Graduate School of Management
Northwestern University

One of the important aspects of this project is the study of the changing characteristics of OR/MS analysts. We have been gathering data on this subject for over four years. Each member of this staff has been asked to fill out this brief, mostly check-off form. We hope that you, too, will be able to help us by filling out this one. Thank you very much.

Your name _____ Organization _____

Title _____ _____

Date _____ _____

A. Education:

School	From	To	Degree	Major	Minor

B. Experience

Organization	Approximate dates		Substantive field: for each job, please check the category that is most appropriate.									Please leave blank				
	from		OR/MS	Mathematics	Teaching	Engineering	Admin.—line	Admin.—staff	Economics	Other	C	M	B	E	O

C. Other education relevant to OR/MS, analysis, and evaluation work.

Subject	Dates	School

D. Publications.

	Yes	No
Book(s)		
Article(s) in referred journals or books		
Contract report(s)		
paper(s) delivered at professional conferences		

E. Please describe briefly your present assignment. Mention, if you can, any projects on which you are now working.

F. GS Grade (optional)

What is your present G.S. grade?_____

What was your G.S. grade when you began doing OR/MS work in government?_____

Notes

Chapter 1
Introduction

1. From Maurice F. Ronayne, "Operations Research Can Help Public Administrators in Decision-Making," *International Review of Administrative Sciences* 3 (1963), reprinted in M. O'Donnell, ed., *Readings in Public Administration* (Boston: Houghton-Mifflin, 1966), p. 141.

2. From *Business and Government Review* (July 1966), reprinted in Ira Sharkansky, ed., *Policy Analysis in Political Science* (Chicago: Markham, 1970), p. 395.

3. "Statement by the President to Cabinet Members and Agency Heads on the New Government-Wide Planning and Budgeting System," August 25, 1965. In *Public Papers of the Presidents of the United States,* Lyndon B. Johnson, 1965, part II, p. 916 (Washington, D.C.: U.S. Government Printing Office, 1966).

4. Root, "The Challenge," in Grace Kelleher, ed., *The Challenge to Systems Analysis* (New York: Wiley, 1970), p. 6, O.R.S.A. Publications in Operations Research #20.

5. "The Genesis of Systems Analysis Within the Bureaucracy." in Kelleher, ed., *The Challenge to Systems Analysis,* p. 9.

6. Ida R. Hoos, "Information Systems and Public Planning," *Management Science* 17:10 (June 1971), pp. B-661-B-662.

7. J. W. Ward and F. M. Burton, abstract of "Environmental Degradation During Construction," paper presented at the XIX-th International Meeting of the Institute of Management Sciences, in *Interfaces*, the Bulletin of the Institute of Management Sciences (March 1972), p. 64.

8. *Ibid.,* pp. 70-71.

9. Wildavsky, "Rescuing Policy Analysis from PPB," in *Public Administration Review* 29:2 (March 1969), pp. 189-202.

10. W. E. Cushen, "Future Demand for Management Science Services in the Federal Government," 1972. This paper will appear in revised form in M. White, M. Radnor, and David A. Tansik, eds., *Management and Policy Science in American Government* (Lexington, Mass.: D. C. Heath, 1975).

11. For the abstracts of specific papers, see *Bulletin of the Operations Research Society of America, Operations Research,* vol. 20, sup. 1 (spring 1972), pp. B-77-B-210.

12. Many early management scientists were scientists, engineers, or mathematicians who taught themselves operations research techniques. See M. Radnor and R. Neal, "The Progress of Management Science Activities in Large U.S. Industrial Corporations," *Operations Research* 21:2 (March 1973) for a discussion of the educational origins of management scientists over a twenty-five-year period in United States business and industry.

13. *WORC Newsletter* 13:5 (January 1974), pp. 4-7.

14. *Public Policymaking Reexamined* (San Francisco: Chandler, 1968), pp. 324-25.

15. *Ibid.,* p. 240.

16. Radnor, "Management Sciences and Policy Sciences," in *Policy Sciences* 2:4 (December 1971), pp. 455-56. Used with permission from Elsevier Scientific Publishing Co.

17. *Ibid.*

18. Dror, *Design for Policy Sciences* (New York: American Elsevier, 1971), p. 12.

19. Radnor, "Management Sciences," p. 448.

Chapter 2
First Steps Toward a Model of the Development and
Adoption of Management Science Activities in
Government Organizations

1. Michael J. White, "The Impact of Management Science on Political Decision-Making," in F. Lyden and E. Miller, eds., *Planning-Programming-Budgeting: A Systems Approach to Management* (Chicago: Markham, 1972); Ida Hoos, "Systems Techniques for Managing Society: A Critique," *Public Administration Review* 33:2 (March 1973); and "Information Systems and Public Planning," *Management Science* 17:10 (June 1971).

2. Michael Radnor, "Stages and Indices of the Evolution of Management Science in Organizations and Their Environments," presented at the Sixteenth International meeting of the Institute of Management Sciences, New York, March 1969; David A. Tansik and Michael Radnor, "An Organization Theory Perspective on the

Development of New Organizational Functions," *Public Administration Review* 31:6 (November 1971).

3. Jan H. B. Huysmans, *The Implementation of Operations Research* (New York: Wiley, 1971).

4. David A. Tansik, *Influences of Organizational Goal Structures on the Selection and Implementation of Management Science Projects,* unpub. Ph.D. diss. Graduate School of Management, Northwestern University, June 1970. Michael Radnor, A. H. Rubenstein, and David A. Tansik, "Implementation in Operations Research and R&D in Government and Business Organizations," *Operations Research* 18:6 (November 1970).

5. C. W. Churchman and A. H. Schainblatt, "The Researcher and the Manager: A Dialectic of Implementation," *Management Science* 11:4 (February 1965).

6. Michael J. White and David A. Tansik, "Implementation of Operations Research in Federal Civilian Agencies: A Field Interview Study," presented at the 41st National Meeting of the Operations Research Society of America, New Orleans, April 1972.

7. Russell L. Ackoff, "Unsuccessful Case Studies and Why," *Operations Research* 8 (1960); "Some Unsolved Problems in Problem-Solving," *Operational Research Quarterly* (U.K.) 13 (1962); D. G. Malcolm, "On the Need for Improvement in Implementation of OR," *Management Science* 11:4 (February 1965).

8. Robert Harris, "The Implementation of Policy Analysis," presented at the National Meeting of the American Society for Public Administration, New York, March 1972.

9. A. H. Rubenstein, "Integration of Operations Research into the Firm," *Journal of Industrial Engineering* 11 (September 1960); A. H. Rubenstein et al., "Some Organizational Factors Related to the Effectiveness of Management Science Groups in Industry," *Management Science* 13:8 (April 1967); Michael Radnor, A. H. Rubenstein, and A. S. Bean, "Integration and Utilization of Management Science Activities in Organizations," *Operational Research Quarterly* (U.K.) 19:2 (June 1968); Radnor "Stages and Indices."

10. C. West Churchman, *The Systems Approach* (New York: Delacort, 1970); E. S. Quade and W. I. Boucher, eds., *Systems Analysis and Policy Planning: Applications to Defense* (New York: American Elsevier, 1968).

11. This discussion is based on the references in note 9.

12. Michael J. White, draft manuscript, June 1968.

13. See the papers by Radnor, Rubenstein, and/or Tansik already cited; Radnor and Neal, "The Progress of Management Science Activities in Large US Industrial Corporations," *Operations Research* 21:2 (March 1973); A. S. Bean et al., "Structural Correlates of Implementation: Success and Failure in U.S. Business Organizations," paper presented at a conference on the Implementation of OR/MS Models, School of Business, University of Pittsburgh, November 15-17, 1973.

14. Melville Dalton, *Men Who Manage* (New York: Wiley, 1959).

15. Kornhauser, with the assistance of Warren O. Hagstrom, *Scientists in Industry: Conflict and Accommodation* (Berkeley: Univ. of California Press, 1962), p. ix.

16. *Ibid.,* p. 157.

17. Berry, "The Short, Happy Life of the Long-Range Planner," *Dun's Review* (January 1967), p. 38. Reprinted by special permission from DUN'S, January, 1967. Copyright, 1967, Dun & Bradstreet Publications Corporation.

18. Tom Burns and G. M. Stalker, *The Management of Innovation* (London: Tavistock, 1961), pp. 90-94, 133-35.

19. Haas, *Beyond the Nation-State* (Stanford: Stanford Univ. Press, 1964), p. 111.

20. Avery, "Enculturation in Industrial Research," *I.R.E. Transactions on Engineering Management* EM-7:1 (March 1960), p. 20. Used by permission of IEEE.

21. *Ibid.*

22. *Ibid.,* p. 22.

23. *Ibid.*

24. Kornhauser, *Scientists in Industry,* pp. 47-48.

25. *Ibid.,* pp. 49, 118ff.

26. *Ibid.,* p. 53.

27. *Ibid.,* pp. 75ff.

28. *Ibid.,* pp. 71ff.

29. *Ibid.,* chap. 3.

30. *Ibid.,* p. 82.

31. *Ibid.*, p. 158.

32. *Ibid.*, p. 175.

33. *Ibid.*, p. 202.

34. LaPorte, "Conditions of Strain and Accommodation in Industrial Research Organizations," *Administrative Science Quarterly* 10:1 (June 1965).

35. Kornhauser, *Scientists in Industry,* pp. 36-37.

36. Schein and Bennis, *Personal and Organizational Change Through Group Methods* (New York: Wiley, 1965), p. 281.

37. *Ibid.*, pp. 278-79.

38. *Ibid.*, p. 283.

39. *Ibid.*, p. 279. Emphasis in original.

40. Rogers, *The Diffusion of Innovations* (Glencoe: Free Press, 1962), pp. 80, 95-98.

41. *Ibid.*, pp. 81ff.

Chapter 3
A Revised Model of the Development of Management Science Activities in Government Agencies

1. Rubenstein, "The Integration of Operations Research into the Firm," *Journal of Industrial Engineering* (September 1960). More recently, Radnor and Neal, "The Progress of Management Science Activities in Large U.S. Industrial Corporations," *Operations Research* 21:2 (March 1973), pp. 433-34.

Chapter 4
Field Methods and Coding

1. Greater detail regarding the material in this chapter is available in Michael J. White, "A Descriptive Model of the Development of Management Science Activities in Federal Civilian Agencies: A Longitudinal, Comparative Field Study with Illustrations," Ph.D. diss., Northwestern University, Evanston, Ill., (June 1974).

2. W.E. Cushen, "The Future Demand for Management Science Services in the Federal Government"(1972). This paper will

appear in revised form in Michael J. White, Michael Radnor, and David A. Tansik. eds., *Management and Policy Science in American Government* (Lexington, Mass.: D.C. Heath, 1975).

3. The personnel data from 1967 to 1968 are compared with similar data gathered in 1971-72 in an unpublished paper by David A. Tansik, Michael Radnor, and Michael J. White, "Trends in the Integration of Management Science Activities in Federal Civilian Agencies," presented at the National Meeting of the Institute of Management Sciences, Houston, Texas, April 1972.

4. The basic concepts in this instrument were derived from E. Mansfield, *The Economics of Technological Change* (New York: W.W. Norton, 1968) and from T. Marschak, T.K. Glennon, and R. Sommers, *A Strategy for R & D* (New York: Springer-Verlag, 1967). Helpful comments were also received from C.F. Douds, M. Radnor, and H. Guetzkow.

Chapter 5
Patterns in the Development of the Adoption and Diffusion of Management Science in Government

1. This is out of forty-six in the sample. The coding of thirty of these is discussed at the end of Chapter 4 and in detail in the appendix to Chapter 4 of Michael J. White, "A Descriptive Model of the Development of Management Science Activities in Federal Civilian Agencies: A Longitudinal Comparative Field Study with Illustrations," Ph.D. diss., Northwestern University, Evanston, Ill., June 1974.

Chapter 6
Management Science and the Study of Organizational Change in Public Administration

1. This discussion is taken from a longer review of social science reaction to management science in my article, "The Impact of Management Science on Political Decision-Making," in F. Lyden and E. Miller, *Planning-Programming-Budgeting: A Systems Approach to Management*, rev. ed. (Chicago: Markham, 1972),

2. Yehezkel Dror briefly summarizes the "pure rationality" model of decision-making in *Public Policymaking Reexamined* (San Francisco: Chandler, 1968). This model is consistent with what Lindblom and others criticize and what some management scientists aspire to as an ideal. See pp. 132-42 in Dror's book.

3. James R. Storey, "Systems Analysis and Welfare Reform," *Policy Sciences* 4:1 (March 1973).

4. *Programming Systems and Foreign Affairs Leadership: An Attempted Innovation* (New York: Oxford Univ. Press, 1970). See also my review of this book in *Policy Sciences* 4:1 (March 1973).

5. A.H. Rubenstein, Michael Radnor, et al., "Some Organizational Factors Related to the Effectiveness of Management Science Groups in Industry," *Management Science* 13:8 (April 1967).

6. Ira S. Lowry, "Reforming Rent Control in New York City," *Policy Sciences* 3:1 (March 1972).

7. Michael Radnor, A.H. Rubenstein, and A.S. Bean, "Integration and Utilization of Management Science Activities in Organizations," *Operation Research Quarterly* (U.K.) 19:2 (June 1968).

8. Radnor and Neal, "The Progress of Management Science Activities in Large U.S. Industrial Corporations," *Operations Research* 21:2 (March 1973).

9. A.S. Bean, R.D. Neal, M. Radnor, and D.A. Tansik, "Structural Correlates of Implementation: Success and Failure in U.S. Business Organizations," paper presented at a research conference on "The Implementation of OR/MS Models: Theory, Research, and Applications," at the Graduate School of Business, University of Pittsburgh, November 1973, revised.

10. Bean, "The Integration of Management Science Activities into Business Organizations," MS thesis, Department of Industrial Engineering and Management Sciences, Northwestern University, Evanston, Ill., August 1969; Bean et al., "Structural Correlates of Implementation."

11. Michael J. White, "Top Management Support and Management Science: An Exploratory Study in 15 Federal Agencies," paper presented at the 1971 Annual Meeting of the American Society for Public Administration, Denver, Colorado, April 1971.

12. Bean, et al., "Structural Correlates of Implementation," pp. 47-54.

13. Tansik, "The Influence of Organizational Goal Structures on the Selection and Implementation of Management Science Projects in Business and Government," in Michael J. White, Michael Radnor, and David A. Tansik, eds., *Management and Policy Science in American Government* (Lexington, Mass.: D.C. Heath, in press).

14. Bean et al., "Structural Correlates of Implementation"; Neal and Radnor, "The Relation Between Formal Procedures for Pursuing OR/MS Activities and OR/MS Group Success," *Operations Research* 21:2 (March 1973).

15. Lowry; Storey; R.E. Park, "The Role of Analysis in Formulating Cable TV Policy," *Policy Sciences 5:1* (March 1973).

16. Detailed citations and further discussion will be found in William Anderson and John M. Gaus, *Research in Public Administration* (Chicago: Public Administration Service, 1945), pp. 12-27. The Macmahon et al., Gaus and Wolcott, and Stone et al. studies were all sponsored by the Social Science Research Council's Committee on Public Administration.

17. Stein, "Introduction," in Stein, ed., *Public Administration and Policy Development* (New York: Harcourt Brace, 1952), p. xxxviii.

18. Ibid., pp. xxii-xxiv.

19. Mosher, "Research in Public Administration: Some Notes and Suggestions," *Public Administration Review* 16:3 (September 1956).

20. Mosher, ed., *Governmental Reorganizations: Cases and Commentary* (Indianapolis: Bobbs-Merrill, 1967).

21. Presthus, *Behavioral Approaches to Public Administration* (University, Ala.: Univ. of Alabama Press, 1965), esp. chaps. 1 and 5.

22. This point is made with references in Michael J. White, "A Descriptive Model of the Development of Management Science Activities in Federal Civilian Agencies: A Longitudinal Comparative Field Study with Illustrations," Ph.D. diss., Northwestern University, Evanston, Ill., (June 1974).

Name Index

Avery, Robert, 15-18

Bean, Alden S., 82ff
Berry, John, 14, 18
Burns, Tom, and G.M. Stalker, 15, 18

Cushen, W.E., 4, 44

Dror, Yehezkel, 5, 6, 80

Fenno, Richard, 80

Gaus, John M., and Leon Wolcott, 85
Gross, Bertram, 80

Haas, Ernst, 15
Hoos, Ida R., 3

Johnson, Lyndon B., 2

Kelleher, Grace J., 3
Kornhauser, William, 14, 16ff

La Porte, Todd, 18
Lindblom, Charles E., 80
Lowry, Ira S., 83, 84

Macmahon, Arthur, John D. Millett, and
    Gladys Ogden, 85

Mosher, Frederick C., 80, 82, 85

Neal, Rodney D., 82, 84

Park, R.E., 84
Presthus, Robert, 86

Radnor, Michael, 5, 7, 10ff, 29, 36, 67, 83ff
Rogers, Everett, 19ff, 40, 71
Ronayne, Maurice F., 2
Root, L. Eugene, 2
Rubenstein, Albert H., 10ff, 29, 36, 37, 67

Schein, Edgar, and Warren Bennis, 19ff
Stein, Harold D., 85
Stockfish, Jacob, 3
Stone, Donald, Don K. Price, and Harold
    Stone, 85
Storey, James, 84

Tansik, David A., 43, 49, 84
Thompson, Victor, 79, 80

Ward, J.W., and F.M. Burton, 3
Weidenbaum, Murray, 2
Wildavsky, Aaron, 4, 80

Subject Index

Accommodation, 9, 13, 14-19, 22
Adoption, 1, 7, 9, 20, 21, 57, 71, 77-78
Aggressiveness, 9, 10, 22, 28-29, 32
Awareness, 20-21

Birth, 10, 16

Capture and record, 85
Case study method, 81, 82ff, 85
Change agent, 19, 21, 32ff, 40, 62ff, 72
Consolidating legitimacy, 21, 28, 32, 40, 58, 62ff, 72ff

Death, 11, 36
Decline, 11, 12
Development-adoption process, 7, 9, 40, 57ff, 71, 77ff, 81, 85
Diffusion, 1, 7, 78, 84

Enculturation, 15ff
Evaluation, 20-21
Evolutionary pattern, 12, 19, 22, 32, 57ff, 72, 73

Forced restructuring, 35, 37, 38, 39, 67

Innovativeness, 9, 15, 22, 27
Institute of Management Sciences, 7, 84
Interest, 20-21
Inter-University Case Program, Inc., 85

Legitimacy, 9, 19, 21, 23, 27, 32
Level of technology, 9, 23, 32, 39-40

Management science, defined, 6-7
Maturity, 11, 67
Missionary, 10, 11, 32, 39, 58
Mutual accommodation, 9, 13, 22

National Society for Corporate Planning, 14
1971 Questionnaire, 50ff, 91-100

Operations research, 2, 4, 5, 25, 46, 79
Operations Research Society of America, 4, 84
Organizationalizing. *See* Forced restructuring

PPBS, 2, 46, 71, 79
Penetration and initial organization, 36-37, 39, 55
Phase changes, 19, 39-40, 55
Policy science, 1, 5, 6
Pre-birth, 10, 36
Processing role, 33-35, 40
Project Complexity Measurement Schedule, 51, 52

Radnor-Rubenstein Model, 9-13, 22, 29, 36, 66
Rand Corporation, 7
Refreezing, 19, 20
Revolutionary pattern, 12, 19, 22, 32-33, 57ff, 71, 73
Routinized change agent role, 33ff, 40, 62, 72

Skills level, 9, 22, 23, 25
Social Science Research Council, 85
Sociotechnical, 40, 57, 77, 78
Southern Regional Training Program, 86
Systems approach, 10

Technical Analysis Division, 4
Top Management Interview Schedule, 51-52
Top management support, 83
Trial, 20, 21

Unfreezing, 19, 20

Washington Operations Research Council, 5

About the Author

Michael J. White is assistant professor of public administration and an associate of the Maxwell Health Studies Program at the Maxwell School of Citizenship and Public Affairs, Syracuse University. He has also been a faculty member of the Universities of Kentucky and Georgia and of the Graduate School of Management at Northwestern University. His interests in organization theory, public budgeting and finance, and management science have led to his coeditorship of *Management and Policy Science in American Government* (Lexington Books, forthcoming 1975) and *Cases in Public Management* (Rand-McNally, 1973), and the authorship of many professional conference papers. Dr. White received the Ph.D. in political science from Northwestern University. He is engaged in research on local government capital budgeting and on hospital financial management.